THE RED BOOK

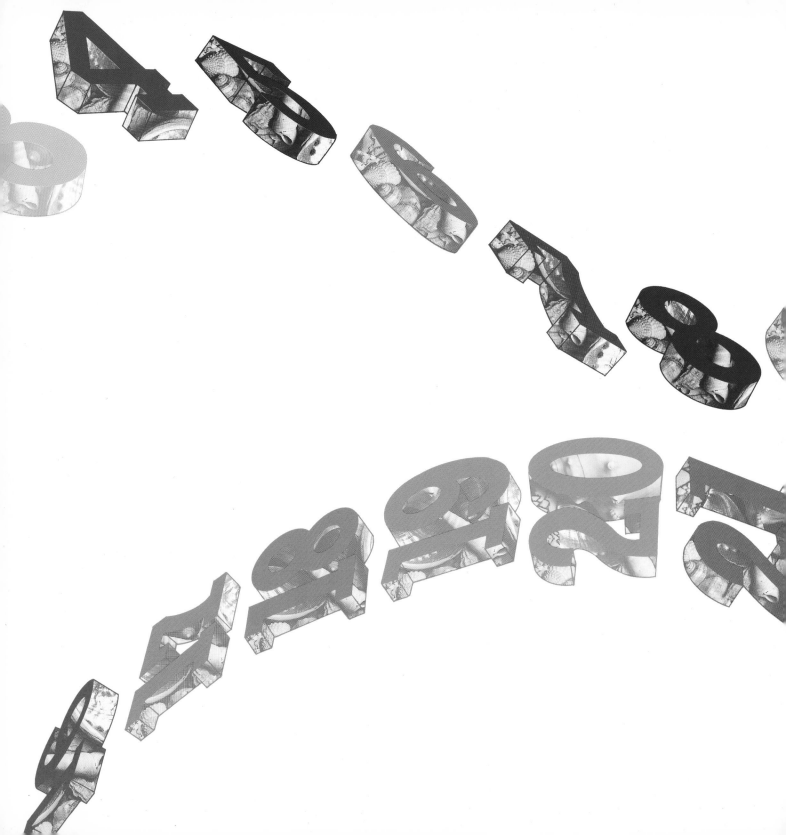

COLORWORKS 1

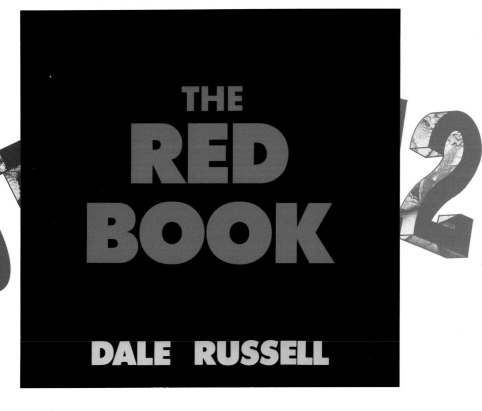

THE
RED
BOOK

DALE RUSSELL

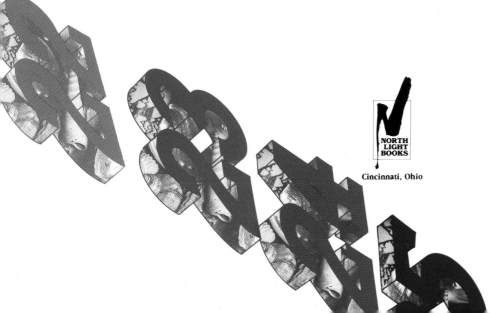

NORTH LIGHT BOOKS

Cincinnati, Ohio

A QUARTO BOOK

ISBN 0-89134-333-4

This book was designed and produced by
Quarto Publishing plc
The Old Brewery
6 Blundell Street
London N7 9BH

SENIOR EDITOR Sally MacEachern
EDITOR Paula Borthwick
DESIGNERS Penny Dawes, David Kemp, Julia King
PICTURE MANAGER: Joanna Wiese
PICTURE RESEARCH CO-ORDINATION Carey Birch,
Prue Reilly, Elizabeth Roberts, Tamara Warner
PHOTOGRAPHERS: Martin Norris, Phil Starling

ART DIRECTOR Moira Clinch
EDITORIAL DIRECTOR Carolyn King

Manufactured in Hong Kong by Regent Publishing Services Ltd
Typeset by Ampersand Typesetting Ltd
Printed in Hong Kong by C & C Joint Printing Co. (H.K.) Ltd

DEDICATION
With great love, I would like to thank my husband Steve for
patiently guiding me through the days and nights overtaken by
color and my daughter Lucy Scarlett for remaining happy
while color came first.

CONTENTS

Using Colorworks

To make the most of the *Colorworks* series it is worthwhile spending some time reading this and the next few pages. *Colorworks* is designed to stimulate a creative use of color. The books do not dictate how color should be applied, but offer advice on how it may be used effectively, giving examples to help generate new ideas. It is essential to remember that *Colorworks* uses the four-color process and that none of the colors or effects use the special brand name ink systems.

The reference system consists of five books that show 125 colors, with 400 type possibilities, 1,000 half-tone options, and 1,500 combinations of color. But even this vast selection should act only as a springboard; the permutations within the books are endless. Use the books as a starting point and experiment!

When choosing colors for graphic design it is almost impossible to predict the finished printed effect. In order to save valuable time spent researching, you can use the series' extensive range of colors to provide references for the shade with which you are working.

The four process colors

Yellow Magenta Cyan Black

▲ Enlarged detail showing how four process colors overlap to produce "realistic" color.

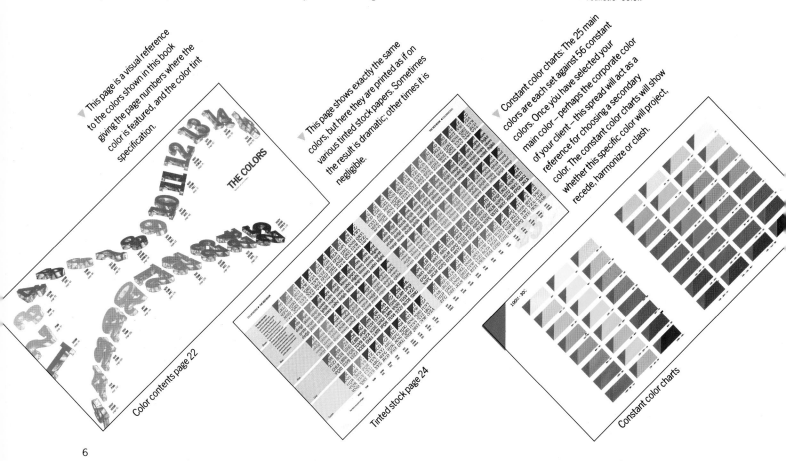

▽ This page is a visual reference to the colors shown in this book giving the page numbers where the color is featured, and the color tint specification.

THE COLORS

Color contents page 22

▽ This page shows exactly the same colors, but here they are printed as if on various tinted stock papers. Sometimes the result is dramatic; other times it is negligible.

Tinted stock page 24

▽ Constant color charts: The 25 main colors are each set against 56 constant colors. Once you have selected your main color – perhaps the corporate color of your client – this spread will act as a reference for choosing a secondary color. The constant color charts will show whether this specific color will project, recede, harmonize or clash.

Constant color charts

The books are ideal for showing to clients who are not used to working with color, so that they may see possible results. They will also be particularly useful when working with a specific color, perhaps dictated by a client's company logo, to see how this will combine with other colors. Equally, when working with several colors dictated by circumstances – and perhaps with combinations one is not happy using – you will find that the constant color charts, colorways and applications will show a variety of interesting solutions. The numerous examples in *Colorworks* can act as a catalyst, enabling you to break out of a mental block – a common problem for designers who may feel that they are using a wide variety of colors but actually be working with a small, tight palette.

Finally, when faced with a direct color choice, you should use *Colorworks* in the same way you would use any other art aid – to help create the final image. The books are designed to administer a shot of adrenaline to the design process. They should be treated as a tool and used as a source of both information and inspiration.

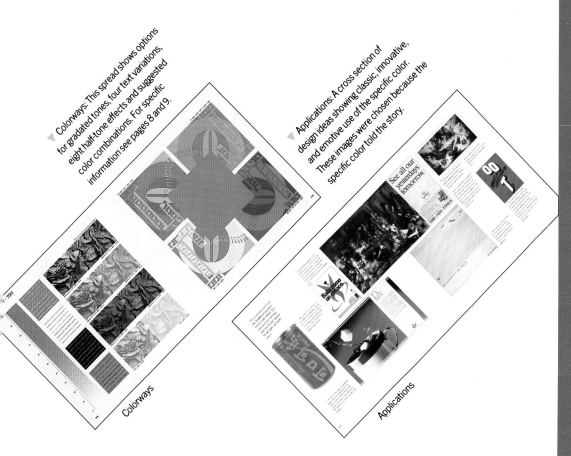

Colorways: This spread shows options for gradated tones, four text variations, eight half-tone effects and suggested color combinations. For specific information see pages 8 and 9.

Applications: A cross section of design ideas showing classic, innovative, and emotive use of the specific color. These images were chosen because the specific color told the story.

Colorways

See all our yesterdays tomorrow.

Applications

On the next four pages you can see, in step-by-step form, exactly how to understand and use the color reference system shown in *Colorworks* and how you can incorporate the ideas into your designs.

It is essential to remember that *Colorworks* uses the four-color process – none of the effects uses the special brand-name ink systems – usually described as "second colors."

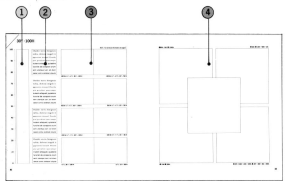

1. GRADATED COLOR

The color scale shows the main color fading from full strength to white. If you are using a gradated background, the scale clearly demonstrates at what point reversed-out type would become illegible – with a dark color you may be able to reverse out down to 20% strength, with a pastel only down to 80%, or perhaps not at all, in which case the type should be produced in a dark color.

The opposite would be true if the design incorporated dark type on a fading dark color. Again, unless a very subtle result is required, the scale indicates at what point type would become illegible.

The other use of the fade gives the designer more color options – perhaps you like the color on page 102, but wish it was slightly paler. With the gradated shading you can visualize just how much paler it could be.

2. TYPE OPTIONS

The main color with different type options; solid with white reversed out; type printing in the color; black and the type reversed out as color; solid with black type. These examples demonstrate the problems of size and tonal values of the type.

The type block is made up of two typefaces, a serif and sans serif, both set in two different sizes.

┌9pt New Baskerville
                          ┌7pt New Baskerville

Ossidet sterio binignuis
gignuntisin stinuand. Flourida

trutent artsquati, quiateire
semi uitantque tueri; sol etiam

└8½pt Univers 55   └7pt Univers 55

Size
Using the four-color process the designer obviously has no problems choosing any combination of tints when using large type, but how small can a specific color type be before it starts to break up or registration becomes a problem? The type block shows when the chosen tints work successfully and more important *when they do not*.

Ossidet sterio binignuis
tultia, dolorat isogult it

9pt New Baskerville 80% Mag demonstrates no problems.

gignuntisin stinuand. Flourida
prat gereafiunt quaecumque

7pt New Baskerville 70% Y 70% M 30% C the serifs start to disappear.

Tonal values
Obviously, when dealing with middle ranges of color, printing the type black or reversed out presents no legibility problems. But the critical decisions are where the chosen colors and shade of type are close. Will black type read on dark green? Will white type reverse out of pale pink? When marking up color, it is always easier to play safe, but using the information in *Colorworks* you will be able to take more risks.

Ossidet sterio binignuis
tultia, dolorat isogult it

Ossidet sterio binignuis
tultia, dolorat isogult it

Ossidet sterio binignuis
tultia, dolorat isogult it

The problem is shown clearly above: using a pastel color (top) it would be inadvisable to reverse type out; with a middle shade (center) the designer can either reverse out or print in a dark color; while using a dark color (bottom), printing type in black would be illegible (or very subtle).

3. HALF-TONE OPTIONS

This section demonstrates some possibilities of adding color to black and white half-tones where the normal, "realistic" four-color reproduction is not desired or when the originals are black and white prints. This section gives the designer 800 options using various percentages and combinations of the process colors.

The mood of the picture can be changed dramatically from hard edged photographs enhanced by a touch of color to pale pastel tints suitable for backgrounds or decorative devices.

Each of the four options are shown using the main color at full strength and at 50% strength. When specifying them to your color separator make sure they understand what you are asking and clearly mark the *percentage* tint of each color that you want. Also, emphasize whether it is a percentage of half-tone or a flat tint that is required.

100% main color   **50% strength of main color**

100% black H/T plus full strength of the main color

100% black H/T plus 50% of the main color

50% black H/T plus full strength of the main color

50% black H/T plus 50% of the main color

100% black H/T plus a *flat* tint of the main color at full strength

100% black H/T plus a *flat* tint of the main color at half strength

H/T using only the main color at full strength

H/T using only the main color at half strength

The photographs (left) have been marked up for origination using options from *Colorworks*. It is unusual to ask for a percentage half-tone – make sure you mark it clearly.

4. COLORWAYS

This page shows the main color with other colors. It acts as a guide to help the designer choose effective color for typography and imagery. Each color is shown as four colorways; each colorway shows the main color with two others.

The three colors in each colorway (corner) are in almost equal proportions. The effect would change dramatically if one color was only a rule or small area. Use the colorways to find the appropriate range for your design and adapt it accordingly.

For information on using the central square and its use in commissioning photography or illustration see page 10.

The choice of color has not been limited to the safe options. The easy neutrals cream, white, and gray have been used, but so have more unusual combinations.

The colors chosen show various effects; look at each corner, if necessary isolating areas.

▽ Colors are shown projecting forward, sometimes using the laws of optics which say that darker, cooler shades recede.

▲ Sometimes, due to the proportions, defying them.

▲ There are classic color combinations.

▲ Colours that are similar in shade.

abcdefghi

▲ Use these colors for background patterns, illustrations or typographic designs where the color emphasis has to be equal.

▲ These colors are not advisable if your design needs to highlight a message.

Analyze your design to see how dominant the typography, illustrations, and embellishments need to be versus the background, then use the colorways to pick the appropriate colors or shades.

When selecting colors, it is very important to eliminate any other color elements that might affect your choice. As has been demonstrated in the color optics section (p14), the character of a color can be dramatically changed by other, adjacent colors.

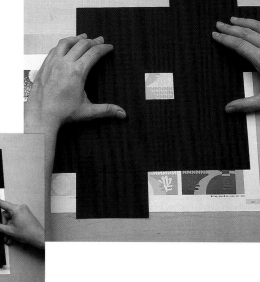

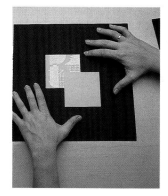

◀▲ The colorways have been designed in such a way that you can mask out the other color options – isolating the area you want to work with or even small sections of each design.

▼▶ The colorways can also be used if you are selecting the color of typography to match/enhance a photograph or illustration; again masking out the other colorways will help. A print of the photograph or illustration can be positioned in the central area, and the mask moved around.

Useful mask shapes

The design shown on this page was created to demonstrate the practical use of *Colorworks*. It combines many half-tone effects and color combinations.

The options illustrated are drawn from *The Red Book*. For more suggestions and further inspiration, refer to the other books in the series.

▶ Using elements from *The Red Book* pages 58-59, 60-61.

◀ Using elements from *The Red Book* 34-35, 36-37.

Red introduction

"*Any of a group of colours, such as that of a ripe tomato or fresh blood, that lie at one end of the visible spectrum, next to orange, and are perceived by the eye when light in the approximate wavelength range 740-620 nanometres falls on the retina. Red is the complementary colour of cyan and forms a set of primary colours with blue and green.*"

Collins English Dictionary; Publishers, William Collins Sons and Co. Ltd., London & Glasgow;
Second Edition 1986

"*A color whose hue resembles that of blood or of the ruby or is that of the long-wave extreme of the visible spectrum.*"

Webster's Ninth New Collegiate Dictionary, Merriam-Webster Inc., Publishers, Springfield,
Massachusetts, U.S.A., 1983

Color is not tangible; it is as fluid as a musical note. Although it may be described, the verbal or written words often bear no relation to its actual form. Color has to be seen in context, for a single shade used in conjunction with another color can take on a whole new character. Searching for a particular shade can be very confusing – somewhat like humming a tune and searching for a forgotten note.

No matter how much theory exists, it is the eye of the designer or artist that is responsible for using color creatively. The fact that color can be rationalized and then break its own rules with complete irrationality is what makes it so fascinating.

This book is about process color. By the very nature of the process system, colors are not blended, as with pigments, but shades are selected visually. Unlike pigment colors, process colors can be mixed without losing any of their chromas. The process primary colors are magenta, yellow, and cyan, with black to create density and contrast, allowing dot saturation to establish values of lightness and darkness. The pigment primaries are red, blue and yellow.

The concept of process color is not really new. The German poet and scientist Goethe (1749-1832) looked at effects of light and darkness on pigment color in a way that strongly relates to modern interpretation of process color. In complete contrast, a practical approach was taken by the 20th-century German painter Hickethier, who created a precise notation system based on cyan, magenta, and yellow for printing. Between these two extremes lies the concept of the process color system.

The colors used in these books had to be systematically chosen to prevent *Colorworks* from dating or the colors from being a purely personal choice. It was important to rely on theory and I finally selected over a thousand colors for the five books that make up this series. This meant working with literally thousands of colors, and yet in spite of this comprehensive palette, there would still be a precise shade that would remain elusive.

Parasols by Raoul Dufy (1877-1953). Dufy has used the tones and hues of a red palette, made all the more dramatic by the complementary green-tinted white. This complementary color reinforces the depth of the dominant reds.

My next major task was to select each image from advertising agencies, design consultancies, illustrators, and actually "off the walls." Every piece of printed matter, label, shopping bag or magazine was a potential gold mine of material for the books. Many images had to be excluded, even though they had superb coloration, because they did not tell a story with one predominant color.

Colorworks examples had to have immediate impact, with one color telling the story – whether in harmony with others, through shock tactics, providing a backdrop, creating a period setting, making instant impact for the recognition of the image content, or simply combining superb color use with design.

Color combinations are infinite, and every day wonderful examples of color and design are being created. Having drawn from just some of these, I hope the *Colorworks* series will be a reference to inspire, confirm, and enjoy.

Dale Russell

Optical illusion, proportion, and texture

The appearance and temperature of red can be changed by minute variations in proportion, surrounding hues, and values of light and darkness, to alter entirely the perception of an image.

Identical red squares will apparently differ in size when given either a light or dark border. It is also possible to change the entire mood or impact of the red hue by surrounding it with a color that is closely related, such as orange. Both shades then take on the same tonal feel and in doing so weaken one another. Conversely, if you were to surround red with a complementary color such as green, the red would be intensified by the red after-image of the green. A similar fluorescent effect can be created by putting proportionally small sections of red on a solid green background.

Red is known to stimulate the nervous system, alerting the senses in proportion to the extent of the exposure. People have been known to become quite agitated when forced to remain for some time in a predominantly red room. Red can be relied upon to play tricks on the eye, just by the merest implication of design, through its direct association with danger, passion, or even parts of the body, such as lips. To create an optical illusion one can rely on psychological association rather than just chromatic interplay.

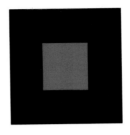

▲ The illusory effect of red is clearly illustrated here, where the red square with a white border looks smaller than that with a black border. When enclosed with a dark color, the red appears lighter and therefore seems to be larger in area, whereas the pale border has the reverse effect.

▲ If you stare at the red dot for a minute and then immediately look at the white area you will see a green dot. This is because red and green are complementary colors.

▲ The solid red oblong in this geometric interplay of colors ensures that the semi-circle cut out forms the 'P', while a subtle gray chevron completes the 'K'. The magenta tinged gray softly enhances the strength of the red, contrasting with the stark black against a white background.

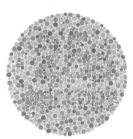

▲ The message formed within the circle of dots is easily read by those with perfect vision, but for those with color blindness, the green dots do not exist. An inability to see green is the most common form of color blindness.

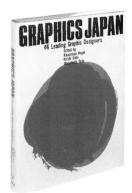

▲ ▲ The use of hues and intensities of red brings life to the Japanese symbol of the sun. Changing the chromatic value of red forms a reaction of light and darkness that gives depth and movement. Placing the red symbol on white enhances this effect, and the sun has the appearance of floating.

▲ A monochrome bowl of fruit beside a red hoop becomes, on second glance, the head of a Carmen Miranda-style Latin American woman. Red is compatible with the geometric design of the black and white, and so the first image – a bowl of fruit – is seen. Then, because of its active nature, red brings the woman to life.

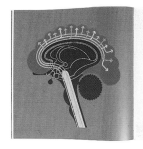

▲ By placing magenta on red with yellow tones and then reversing the process, as seen with the letters W and X, two completely different effects are created. In the first example there is a pleasing tonal similarity; because of the volume of red, the magenta is subdued and becomes a warm tone. However, when the colors are reversed, as with the letter X, there is a 3D, clashing image. The magenta background makes the yellow tones in the red stronger, creating a more vivid impression.

▲ A red background for white typography not only gives the logo impact but actually has the effect of projecting the words. The brightness of the red also makes the teal background of the main image appear to recede and therefore highlights the 3D "floating face." A bridge is created between the logo typography and Jean Paul Gaultier's pale image by the strong use of red.

The red tab placed on the right effectively brings the eye to the black print at the bottom of the page, and so as not to diminish the impact of the main 3D effect, it is counterbalanced by the use of black.

▲ ▲ The use of magenta behind the main image, clashing with the red background, not only has impact but, in conjunction with the pastel arrows, creates the illusion of movement. What would have been a passive illustration becomes vibrant through the use of magenta and red.

▲ One sees a head wearing a top hat, and yet all there is on the page to tell us this is a red dot and a black hat. The use of red rather than pink for the nose makes this image recognizable as the American entertainer W. C. Fields, who was known for his red nose.

▲ The textured effect is achieved not only by the graphic design of the calendar page but also by the tonal use of two shades of red within the central core of the illustration. The effect is intensified by using a different shade of red to shadow the main image, forming a 3D impression.

▲ An electric combination of tonally similar colors has immediate impact as the proportionally small amount of red leaps out of the solid blue background.

Psychology

Red has a number of strongly emotive and
sometimes contradictory connotations
which include danger, passion, anger, fire,
sex, and blood. The hot-blooded, sexy
image of red lipstick and red lights contrasts
sharply with the religious association of the
red communion wine with the blood of
Jesus.

Popular Western catchphrases abound with red
imagery; for example "to see red" refers to
blood rushing behind the eyes during a fit of
anger; "red rag to a bull" refers to something
that has caused outrage; to "paint the town
red" is to have a riotous time; you are
"caught red-handed" when found with the
blood of a crime still on your hands. There is
also the infamous "scarlet woman," which is
how the Bible describes a sinful woman.

Red has such a strong association with heat that
it is possible to feel warmer when in a red
environment even though the temperature
has not changed.

The use of red, with other colors, for packaging,
is psychologically effective on various levels:
it has an illusory effect of "advancing"
toward the buyer, it attracts attention, and
because it is a strong color it makes a
positive statement about the product.

🔺 The old colloquialism "to
roll out the red carpet" is
applied literally in this British
Airways advertisement. A
large area of red in the page
design reinforces the
association with important
people and regal treatment.

🔺 With the use of red for the
typography, the word
"turquoise" loses its meaning.
The red is so dominant that
one sees the word and
registers a slightly disturbing
color image. It is only on
reflection that you realize that
if the colors of the typography
and clothing were
transposed, this would be a
conventional picture.

🔺 Night and day are simply
represented by the basic
associations of colors and
shapes. The full chromatic
use of red and yellow against
the equally solid backgrounds
graphically illustrates that the
store is open day and night.

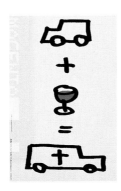

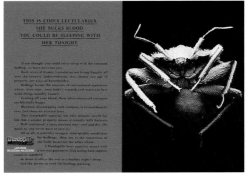

▲ ▲ Blood appears to be pouring from the monochrome fur coat. This is red at its most shockingly emotive, designed for intense impact by the use of a white background and monochrome graphics.

▲ Hues and intensity are combined with the emotive connotations of the colors to produce a visual effect. Red has the immediate impact of fire, and black represents iron. Typography and a blending of color weld the two concepts and create a whole image.

▲ ▲ In this case red is associated with both wine and blood . The **severity** of the message "Don't drink and drive" is strengthened by the childlike simplicity of the graphics. The use of black on white further emphasizes the impact of the red wine in the glass, which could also be a splash of blood on the page.

▲ We have instinctively learned to react to red as a danger signal. By giving road signs a red border, highway authorities alert drivers to read the sign. Reliance on the psychological impact of red for danger is applied to numerous warning signs in which stopping or slowing down is the issue. (detail from image by Pentagram)

▲ A psychological approach to this advertising campaign for mattresses uses horror tactics to implant the message. Placing the text on solid red against black and white gives the strongest possible visual impact. The psychological message is fear – the graphic red background states that the bedbug is connected with blood. The text "she sucks blood" reinforces the association.

▲ ▲ The festive use of the "wrong" color combinations in this pastiche of Gitanes cigarettes creates an eyecatching party invitation. Red hues and magenta were cleverly chosen for their association with passion, wine, and action.

Marketing

Red is effective as a marketing tool in a number of different ways. It is a high-profile color and is extremely eyecatching, especially when used as a "flash" on packaging. It creates an aura of activity and energy and is strongly emotive, attracting all ages and both sexes.

Completely different perspectives can be created by using red in a variety of color combinations. Even when working with just two colors and changing only their tonal effect, you can achieve two opposite images. For example, in the advertisement for Red Stripe Lager, a red stripe evokes a free, bohemian lifestyle. Yet the red Marlborough cigarette pack is associated with an active outdoor life. The same red tells two different stories. Simply by changing the tonal surroundings the marketing team are able to encourage the relevant psychological reaction necessary from numerous documented associations with the color red.

Within the red spectrum, magenta – combined with colors such as lime or orange to create a fluorescent effect – generally appeals to a younger market. Terracotta will attract a sophisticated consumer, aubergine purple is avantgarde and maroon is considered a safe color.

However, no matter how many color theories exist, by the very nature of chroma and hue, the slightest change or addition of a combined shade can create an image or atmosphere appropriate to an entirely different market.

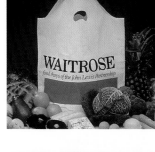

▲ ▲ The red of the Marlborough cigarette pack when placed within the setting of a conventional monochrome photograph has associations of virility, strength and an active outdoor life.

▲ A red stripe on a muted black and white grained image creates a sense of Soho – London or New York – a life of bars and jazz, a free bohemian life style.

▲ ▲ The choice of an earth color for the shopping bag harmonizes with the colors of the fresh, homegrown vegetables and fruit, newly baked bread, and dairy produce. By tastefully using this discreet shade of terracotta against the neat, clean lines of black on white, the company is appealing to middle-class customers who expect good quality and value.

▲ This classic combination of maroon and gold is both traditional and festive. This rich shade has connotations of quality and an opulence which is enhanced by the fine gold script; all entirely in keeping with the company and the discriminating purchasers of its products.

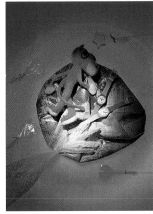

▲ To capture the attention of a younger market, magenta and blue visual imagery link content and color. Magenta forms a spotlight around the central contents, and the glow of the magenta is strengthened by the surrounding tonal blue.

▲▲ The combination of colors and patterns is compatible with a specific movement in 1989 British youth culture. There is a "flower power" effect on the red-hued compact disc which contrasts tonally with the purist lilac cover. The puce tie features starkly on the white shirt and red jacket but forms a bridge between the lilac and the positive red inside cover.

▲ The red wrapper of the popsicle appeals to all ages. It relies on the impact of cherry red incorporated with the secondary colors to promote the product. It is apparent from the wrapper that the flavor is that of fresh, juicy cherries.

▲ The bold use of red, in conjunction with white and the silver foil, creates a crisp, clean image which in no way alludes to chocolate but has a refreshing appeal. By using bright red the product is aimed at the entire market, rather than at just one segment.

▲ This image gives the impression of a top-quality product. The red seal applied to the cream wrapping suggests that the dairy products have been individually approved and prepared, and the combination has a "French" flavor. The minimal use of red for the stripe and seal, together with the elegant, light black calligraphy on a cream background, is wonderfully chic and will appeal to a sophisticated and discerning customer.

19

Culture and period

Different cultures interpret red in a variety of ways. In China red is a wedding color; it represents good luck but is also the color for jealousy (unlike in the West, where green symbolizes jealousy). In India red represents chivalry and the red mark placed on a woman's forehead at her wedding by her father represents his blood and is a blessing intended to produce heroic and courageous children.

Red, perhaps more than any other color, has nationalistic implications, as it features in the flags of countries around the world. A clever application or addition of red within a design can ensure that a particular image is associated with a specific country.

Different cultures may have their own interpretations of color, but there are some associations that are universal: red will always be connected with heat, blood, emotion, and danger. Equally, over the ages certain colors have become identified with particular times when they were in popular use. For example, ruby is known as a Victorian color, Regency red is so named for its connection with that period of British history, and magenta hues are identified with the 1930s.

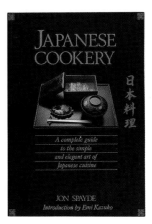

▲▲ Italy is instantly evoked through the use of red and green, echoing the colors of the country's flag. The nationalistic coloration brings life and movement to the graphic application of the typography.

▲ The minimalist design of the lacquer black book cover is brought to life by a touch of red. This cleverly evokes the red of the Japanese flag, as well as toning with the lacquer red of the dish – an effective combination of traditional elements with modern design.

▲ The use of shocking pink and bright yellow in conjunction with cross-hatching suggests the atmosphere of a Georgian theatrical sketch, giving a sense of period to this illustration. Continuing the bright pink on the information graphics reinforces the overall image of a "pink page" in a calendar devoted to color.

SYLVIA PLATH

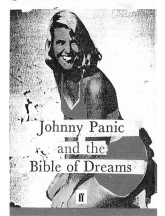

Johnny Panic
and the
Bible of Dreams

▲ The skin and hair tones of this 1950s image are tinted in a style typical of the time. The chromatic red of the bikini and bottom border manages to maintain the period feeling but also makes the book cover eyecatching and relevant for the late 1980s.

▲ Post-war French intellectualism is conveyed not only through the graphics style but also through the magenta tinting of monochrome images popular during this period. The clothing reveals that the period is actually late 1950s, but the whole poster has a modern approach characteristic of the late 1980s.

▲ This compendium of games is a careful reproduction of Victorian life. The use of marbled hues of ruby red, so typical of Victorian decoration, creates the aura of gentility and superior craftsmanship. This is a clever interpretation of the colors and graphics of a bygone era nostalgically viewed from the eighties.

▲ Time gaps between cultures and their associated colors are becoming shorter, to the extent that colors that were synonymous with the 1960s have made a comeback, albeit in a different guise, in the late 1980s. Drug culture has a definite association with both eras and the optical illusion created by these bright colors recreates the effect of hallucinogenic drugs. Magenta, when used as a background for the other colors, creates a fluorescent illusion, and the image is typical of the Acid House following of the eighties.

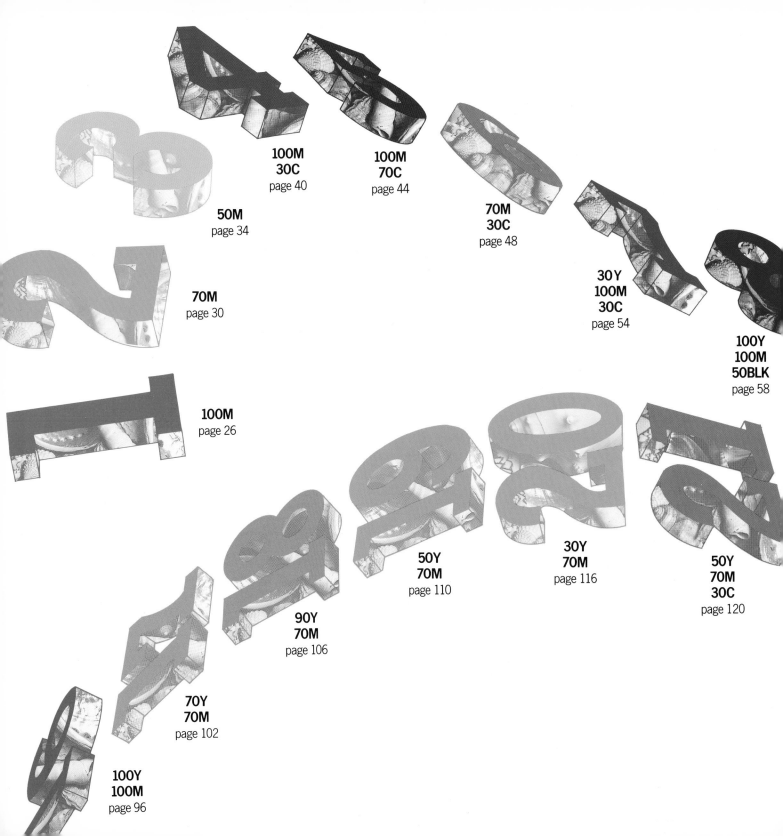

50M
page 34

100M
30C
page 40

100M
70C
page 44

70M
30C
page 48

30 Y
100M
30C
page 54

100Y
100M
50BLK
page 58

70M
page 30

100M
page 26

50Y
70M
page 110

30Y
70M
page 116

50Y
70M
30C
page 120

90Y
70M
page 106

70Y
70M
page 102

100Y
100M
page 96

30Y
100M
page 80

40Y
100M
10BLK
page 76

50Y
100M
page 86

60Y
100M
70C
page 72

70Y
100M
page 90

50Y
100M
30C
page 68

30Y
70M
30C
page 62

THE COLORS

Numbers are percentages

70Y
70M
30C
page 124

100Y
100M
30C
page 130

70Y
100M
50C
page 134

100Y
100M
70BLK
page 138

23

COLORS ON TINTS

The 25 main colors are printed on background tints to simulate the effect of printing color on printed stock. This chart can be used in a number of ways: as a guide to see how pale your chosen color can go before it merges with the printed stock; to determine the aesthetic advantages of using a particular color on a specific stock and to experiment with subtle patterns.

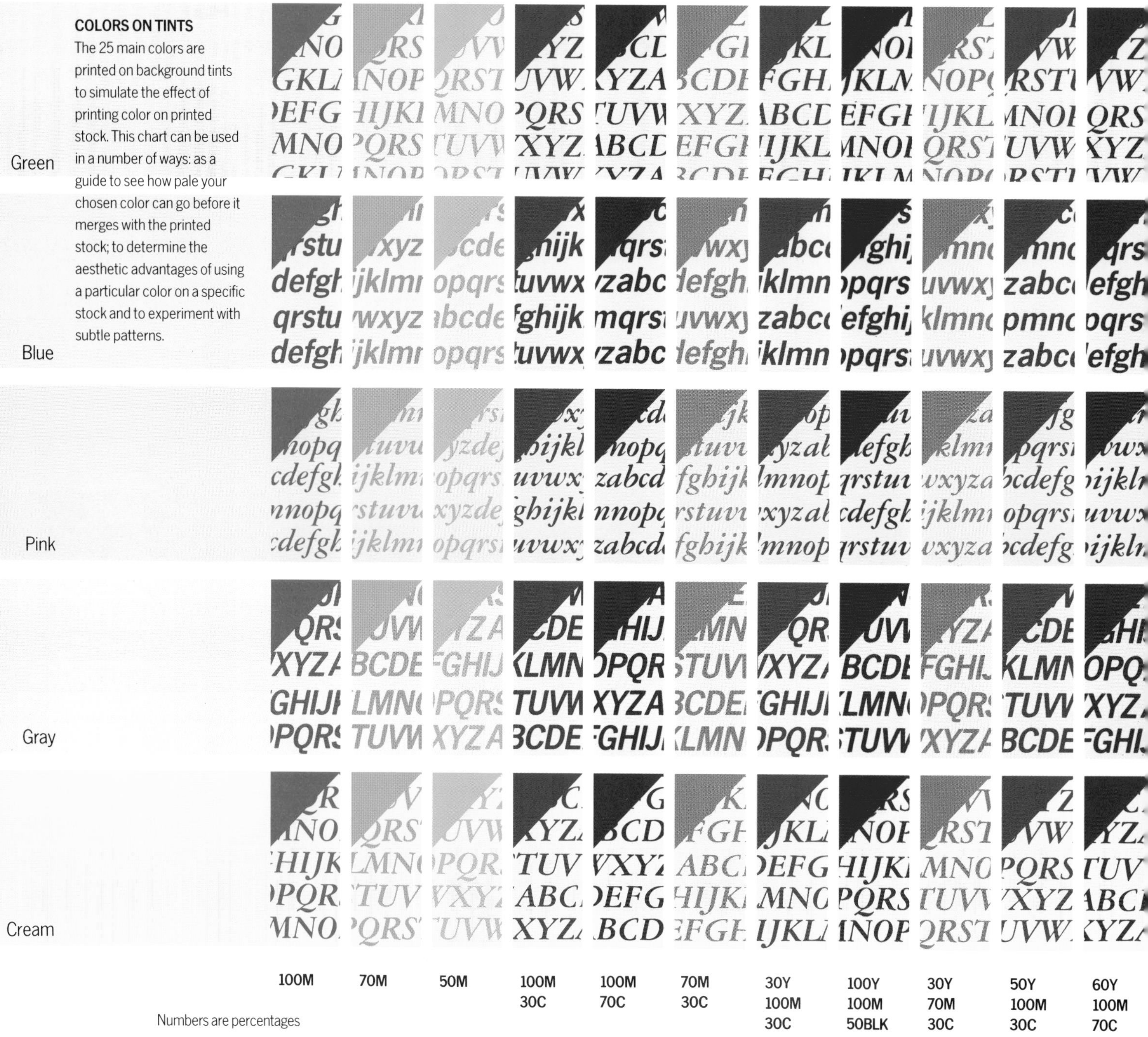

Green

Blue

Pink

Gray

Cream

| 100M | 70M | 50M | 100M 30C | 100M 70C | 70M 30C | 30Y 100M 30C | 100Y 100M 50BLK | 30Y 70M 30C | 50Y 100M 30C | 60Y 100M 70C |

Numbers are percentages

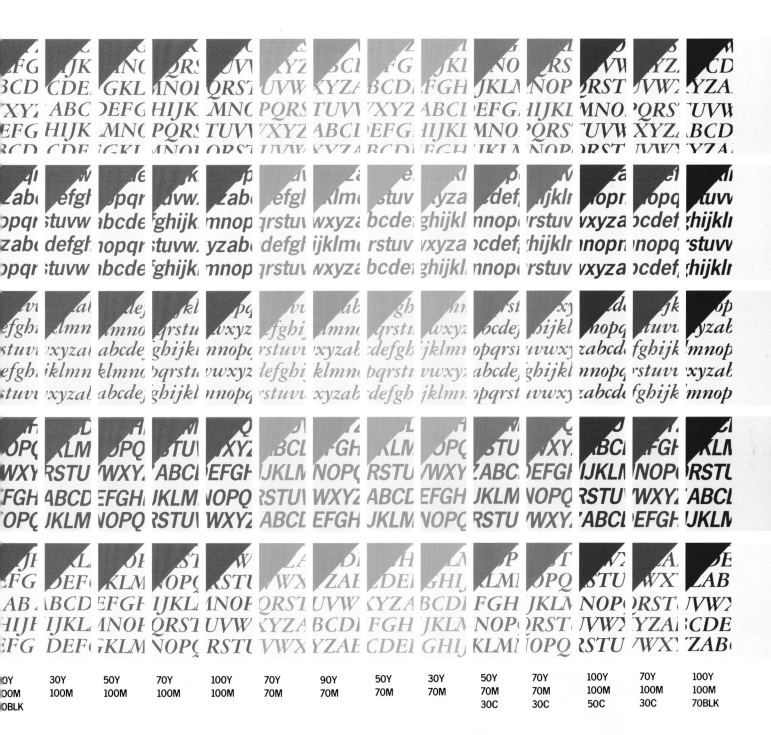

0Y	30Y	50Y	70Y	100Y	70Y	90Y	50Y	30Y	50Y	70Y	100Y	70Y	100Y
00M	100M	100M	100M	100M	70M	70M	70M	70M	70M	70M	100M	100M	100M
0BLK									30C	30C	50C	30C	70BLK

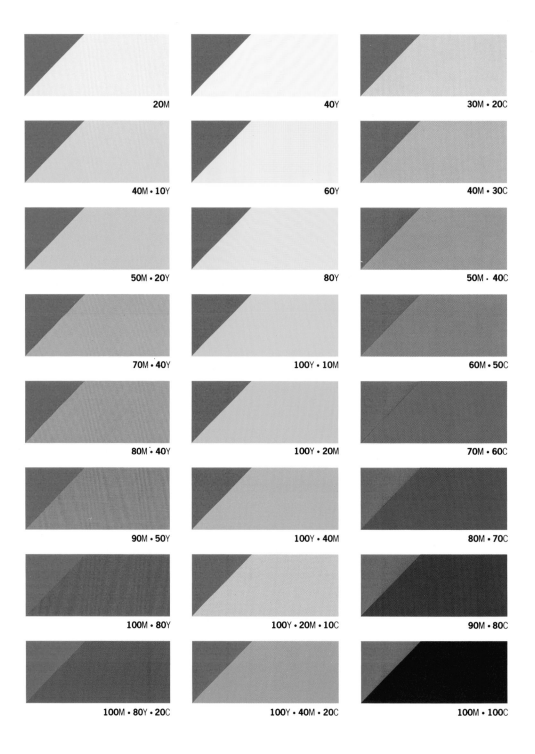

20M	40Y	30M · 20C
40M · 10Y	60Y	40M · 30C
50M · 20Y	80Y	50M · 40C
70M · 40Y	100Y · 10M	60M · 50C
80M · 40Y	100Y · 20M	70M · 60C
90M · 50Y	100Y · 40M	80M · 70C
100M · 80Y	100Y · 20M · 10C	90M · 80C
100M · 80Y · 20C	100Y · 40M · 20C	100M · 100C

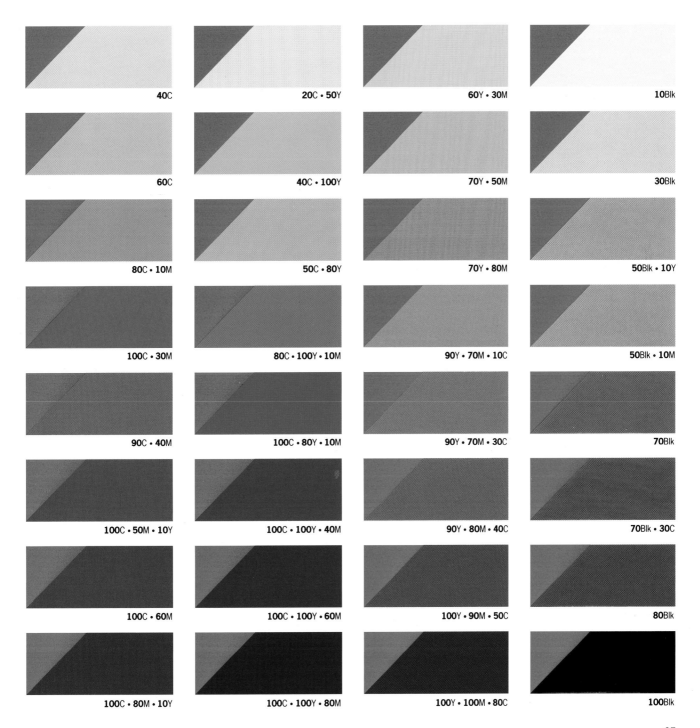

40C

20C • 50Y

60Y • 30M

10Blk

60C

40C • 100Y

70Y • 50M

30Blk

80C • 10M

50C • 80Y

70Y • 80M

50Blk • 10Y

100C • 30M

80C • 100Y • 10M

90Y • 70M • 10C

50Blk • 10M

90C • 40M

100C • 80Y • 10M

90Y • 70M • 30C

70Blk

100C • 50M • 10Y

100C • 100Y • 40M

90Y • 80M • 40C

70Blk • 30C

100C • 60M

100C • 100Y • 60M

100Y • 90M • 50C

80Blk

100C • 80M • 10Y

100C • 100Y • 80M

100Y • 100M • 80C

100Blk

100
90
80
70
60
50
40
30
20
10
0

Ossidet sterio binignuis
tultia, dolorat isogult it
gignuntisin stinuand. Flourida
prat gereafiunt quaecumque
trutent artsquati, quiateire
lurorist de corspore orum
semi uitantque tueri; sol etiam
caecat contra osidetsal utiquite

Ossidet sterio binignuis
tultia, dolorat isogult it
gignuntisin stinuand. Flourida
prat gereafiunt quaecumque
trutent artsquati, quiateire
lurorist de corspore orum
semi uitantque tueri; sol etiam
caecat contra osidetsal utiquite

Ossidet sterio binignuis
tultia, dolorat isogult it
gignuntisin stinuand. Flourida
prat gereafiunt quaecumque
trutent artsquati, quiateire
lurorist de corspore orum
semi uitantque tueri; sol etiam
caecat contra osidetsal utiquite

Ossidet sterio binignuis
tultia, dolorat isogult it
gignuntisin stinuand. Flourida
prat gereafiunt quaecumque
trutent artsquati, quiateire
lurorist de corspore orum
semi uitantque tueri; sol etiam
caecat contra osidetsal utiquite

NOTE: For technical information see page 6

100 Blk H/T • H/T's: **100** M   **100** Blk H/T • H/T's: **50** M

50 Blk H/T • H/T's: **100** M   **50** Blk H/T • H/T's: **50** M

100 Blk H/T • F/T's: **100** M   **100** Blk H/T • F/T's: **50** M

H/T's: **100** M   H/T's: **50** M

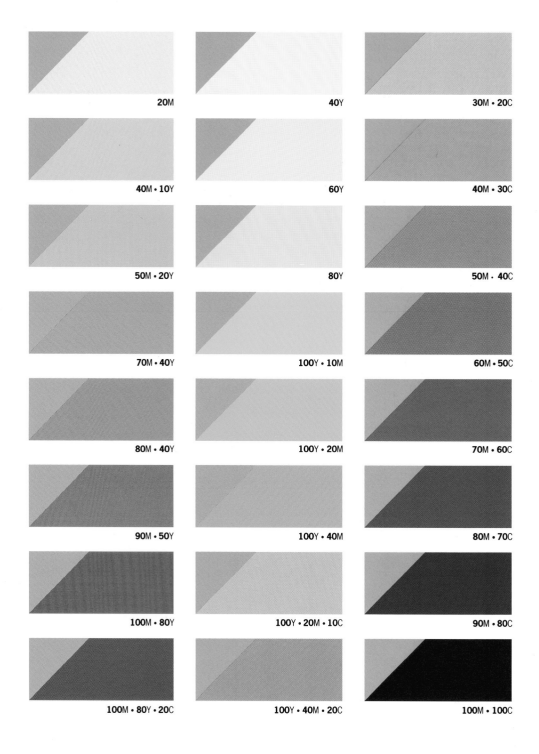

20M

40Y

30M • 20C

40M • 10Y

60Y

40M • 30C

50M • 20Y

80Y

50M • 40C

70M • 40Y

100Y • 10M

60M • 50C

80M • 40Y

100Y • 20M

70M • 60C

90M • 50Y

100Y • 40M

80M • 70C

100M • 80Y

100Y • 20M • 10C

90M • 80C

100M • 80Y • 20C

100Y • 40M • 20C

100M • 100C

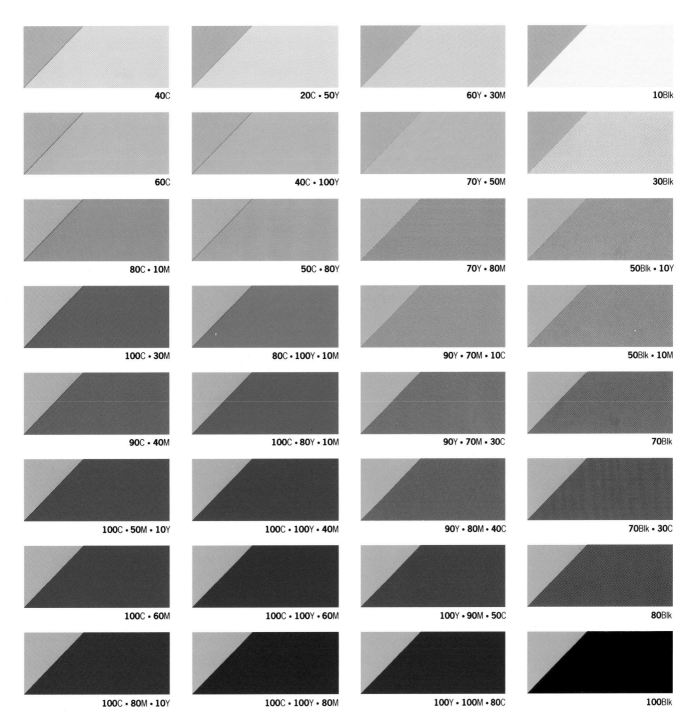

40C	20C • 50Y	60Y • 30M	10Blk
60C	40C • 100Y	70Y • 50M	30Blk
80C • 10M	50C • 80Y	70Y • 80M	50Blk • 10Y
100C • 30M	80C • 100Y • 10M	90Y • 70M • 10C	50Blk • 10M
90C • 40M	100C • 80Y • 10M	90Y • 70M • 30C	70Blk
100C • 50M • 10Y	100C • 100Y • 40M	90Y • 80M • 40C	70Blk • 30C
100C • 60M	100C • 100Y • 60M	100Y • 90M • 50C	80Blk
100C • 80M • 10Y	100C • 100Y • 80M	100Y • 100M • 80C	100Blk

NOTE: For technical information see page 6

Ossidet sterio binignuis tultia, dolorat isogult it gignuntisin stinuand. Flourida prat gereafiunt quaecumque trutent artsquati, quiateire lurorist de corspore orum semi uitantque tueri; sol etiam caecat contra osidetsal utiquite

100 Blk H/T • H/T's: **70** M   **100** Blk H/T • H/T's: **35** M

Ossidet sterio binignuis tultia, dolorat isogult it gignuntisin stinuand. Flourida prat gereafiunt quaecumque trutent artsquati, quiateire lurorist de corspore orum semi uitantque tueri; sol etiam caecat contra osidetsal utiquite

50 Blk H/T • H/T's:**70** M   **50** Blk H/T • H/T's: **35** M

Ossidet sterio binignuis tultia, dolorat isogult it gignuntisin stinuand. Flourida prat gereafiunt quaecumque trutent artsquati, quiateire lurorist de corspore orum semi uitantque tueri; sol etiam caecat contra osidetsal utiquite

100 Blk H/T • F/T's: **70** M   **100** Blk H/T • F/T's: **35**M

Ossidet sterio binignuis tultia, dolorat isogult it gignuntisin stinuand. Flourida prat gereafiunt quaecumque trutent artsquati, quiateire lurorist de corspore orum semi uitantque tueri; sol etiam caecat contra osidetsal utiquite

H/T's: **70** M   H/T's: **35** M

■ 70M • 50C ■ 20Y • 20M • 10C

■ 80M • 40C ■ 40Y • 70C

10Blk ■ 20Y • 20M • 10C • 10Blk

■ 100Blk ■ 10Y • 20M • 20Blk

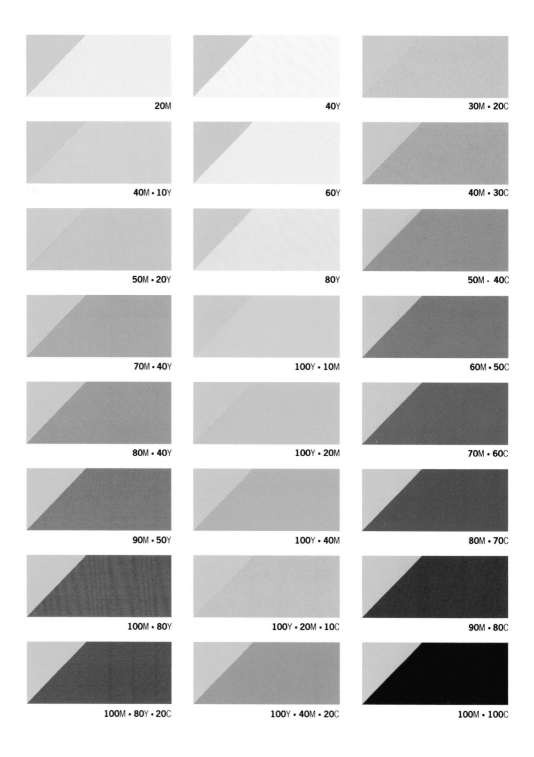

20M

40Y

30M · 20C

40M · 10Y

60Y

40M · 30C

50M · 20Y

80Y

50M · 40C

70M · 40Y

100Y · 10M

60M · 50C

80M · 40Y

100Y · 20M

70M · 60C

90M · 50Y

100Y · 40M

80M · 70C

100M · 80Y

100Y · 20M · 10C

90M · 80C

100M · 80Y · 20C

100Y · 40M · 20C

100M · 100C

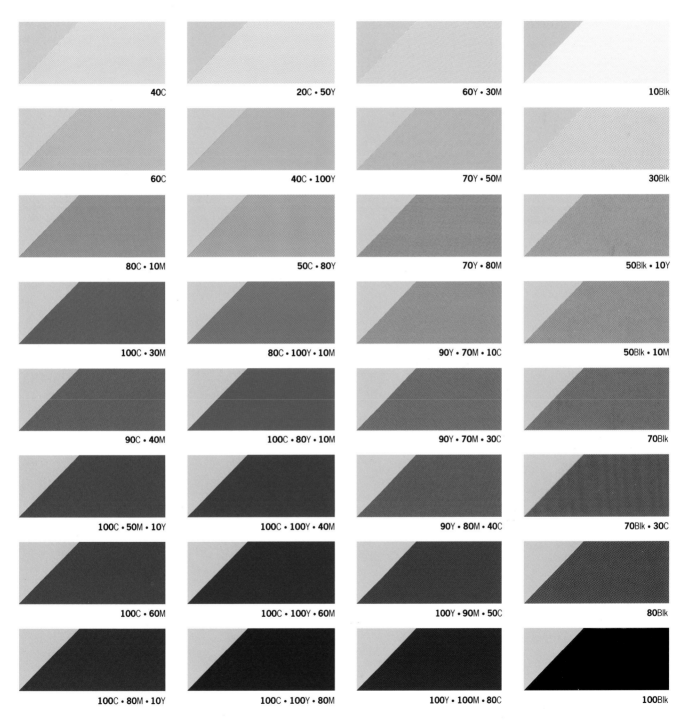

40C

20C • 50Y

60Y • 30M

10Blk

60C

40C • 100Y

70Y • 50M

30Blk

80C • 10M

50C • 80Y

70Y • 80M

50Blk • 10Y

100C • 30M

80C • 100Y • 10M

90Y • 70M • 10C

50Blk • 10M

90C • 40M

100C • 80Y • 10M

90Y • 70M • 30C

70Blk

100C • 50M • 10Y

100C • 100Y • 40M

90Y • 80M • 40C

70Blk • 30C

100C • 60M

100C • 100Y • 60M

100Y • 90M • 50C

80Blk

100C • 80M • 10Y

100C • 100Y • 80M

100Y • 100M • 80C

100Blk

NOTE: For technical information see page 6

100
90
80
70
60
50
40
30
20
10
0

Ossidet sterio binignuis tultia, dolorat isogult it gignuntisin stinuand. Flourida prat gereafiunt quaecumque trutent artsquati, quiateire lurorist de corspore orum semi uitantque tueri; sol etiam caecat contra osidetsal utiquite

Ossidet sterio binignuis tultia, dolorat isogult it gignuntisin stinuand. Flourida prat gereafiunt quaecumque trutent artsquati, quiateire lurorist de corspore orum semi uitantque tueri; sol etiam caecat contra osidetsal utiquite

Ossidet sterio binignuis tultia, dolorat isogult it gignuntisin stinuand. Flourida prat gereafiunt quaecumque trutent artsquati, quiateire lurorist de corspore orum semi uitantque tueri; sol etiam caecat contra osidetsal utiquite

Ossidet sterio binignuis tultia, dolorat isogult it gignuntisin stinuand. Flourida prat gereafiunt quaecumque trutent artsquati, quiateire lurorist de corspore orum semi uitantque tueri; sol etiam caecat contra osidetsal utiquite

100 Blk H/T • H/T's: **50** M   100 Blk H/T • H/T's: **25** M

50 Blk H/T • H/T's: **50** M   50 Blk H/T • H/T's: **25** M

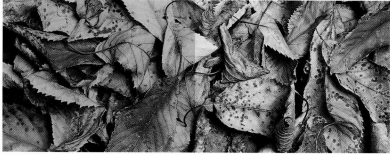

100 Blk H/T • F/T's: **50** M   100 Blk H/T • F/T's: **25** M

H/T's: **50** M   H/T's: **25** M

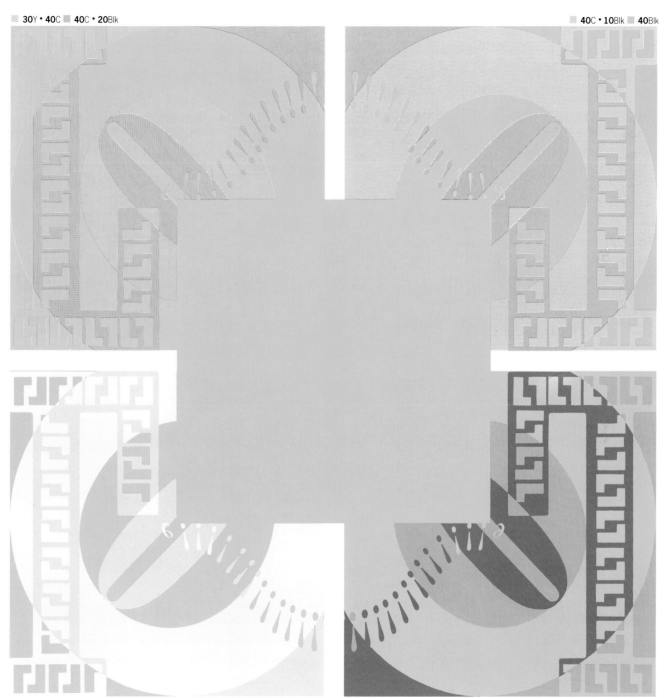

Magenta is a living color. It is confident, clashing, fluorescent and even vulgar depending on how it is applied. Magenta is one of the three primary colors in the four color process.

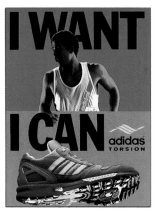

▲ The tonally subdued green behind the statement "I want" gives the illusion of holding back, while the more assertive magenta creates a foreground which enables the positive statement "I can" to leap forward.

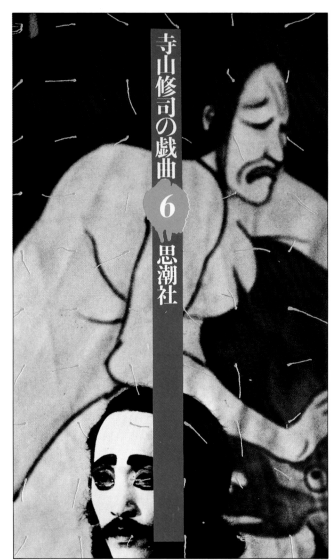

▼ The predominant magenta of the illustration is cleverly matched in the typography, allowing the atmosphere created in the picture to fill the entire page. This shade of magenta reinforces the image of a warm, sun-soaked southern France and provides continuity between type and imagery.

▲ The monochrome Japanese collage with blue banner is brought to life by the use of pink overlay flecks, which give a feeling of movement to a primarily harsh image. The lively pink is then used again as a central seal to catch the eye and draw instant attention to the number 6.

▷ The notion of liberation is effectively highlighted here by a bold yet gentle shade of pink which contrasts strongly with the black barbed wire.

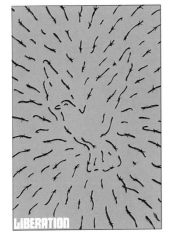

LIBERATION

NOVA

▷ The combination of colors and a nonconformist design turns this into a vulgar pink. Using the pink as an erratically defined background and for the typography makes the album cover for the punk rock group "Sex Pistols" crudely defiant. This strong color combination has a cult tradition and follows on from, among others, Andy Warhol.

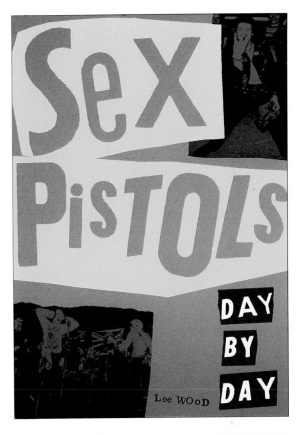

SeX PiSTOLS

DAY BY DAY

Lee WOoD

▲ The visual message of the magazine cover is described in the typography: "Think pink and the world will look rosy." The effect is achieved by the striking magenta title, caption, and model's makeup, set against a white background. The clashing red of the intermediate statements provides a counterbalance, but the overall statement remains magenta.

▷ The confident use of magenta for the model's makeup and clothing, duplicating the magenta of the Evian water label and toning with the blue, allows a minimalist approach to the product, reinforcing the statement, "So pure there's almost nothing to it."

SO PURE THERE'S ALMOST NOTHING TO IT

evian

eau minérale naturelle des Alpes françaises.

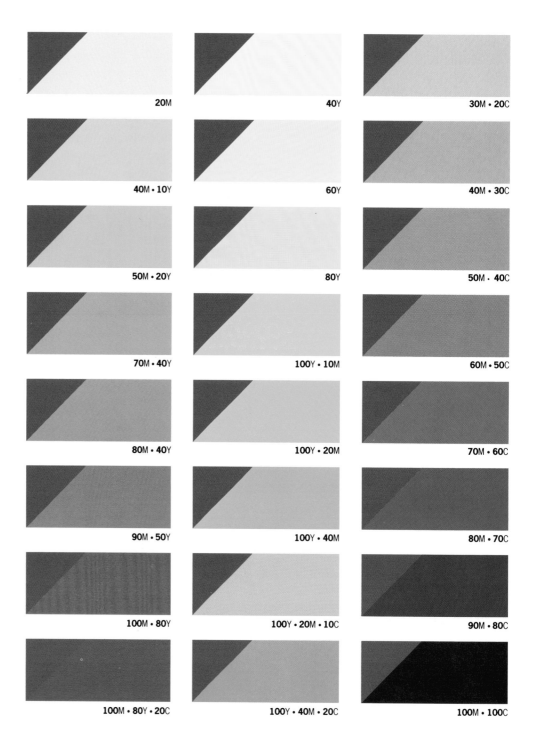

20M

40Y

30M · 20C

40M · 10Y

60Y

40M · 30C

50M · 20Y

80Y

50M · 40C

70M · 40Y

100Y · 10M

60M · 50C

80M · 40Y

100Y · 20M

70M · 60C

90M · 50Y

100Y · 40M

80M · 70C

100M · 80Y

100Y · 20M · 10C

90M · 80C

100M · 80Y · 20C

100Y · 40M · 20C

100M · 100C

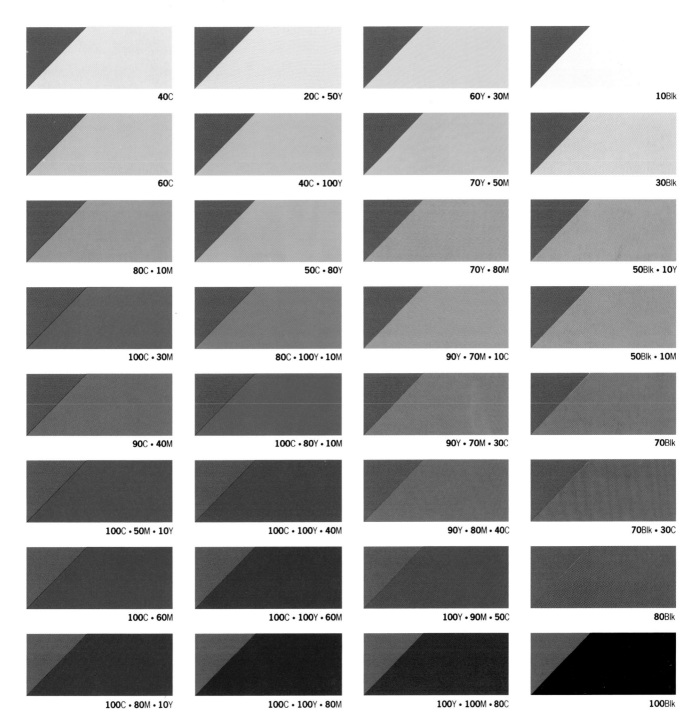

40C

20C · 50Y

60Y · 30M

10Blk

60C

40C · 100Y

70Y · 50M

30Blk

80C · 10M

50C · 80Y

70Y · 80M

50Blk · 10Y

100C · 30M

80C · 100Y · 10M

90Y · 70M · 10C

50Blk · 10M

90C · 40M

100C · 80Y · 10M

90Y · 70M · 30C

70Blk

100C · 50M · 10Y

100C · 100Y · 40M

90Y · 80M · 40C

70Blk · 30C

100C · 60M

100C · 100Y · 60M

100Y · 90M · 50C

80Blk

100C · 80M · 10Y

100C · 100Y · 80M

100Y · 100M · 80C

100Blk

100M · 30C

NOTE: For technical information see page 6

| 100 |
| 90 |
| 80 |
| 70 |
| 60 |
| 50 |
| 40 |
| 30 |
| 20 |
| 10 |
| 0 |

Ossidet sterio binignuis tultia, dolorat isogult it gignuntisin stinuand. Flourida prat gereafiunt quaecumque **trutent artsquati, quiateire lurorist de corspore orum** semi uitantque tueri; sol etiam caecat contra osidetsal utiquite

Ossidet sterio binignuis tultia, dolorat isogult it gignuntisin stinuand. Flourida prat gereafiunt quaecumque **trutent artsquati, quiateire lurorist de corspore orum** semi uitantque tueri; sol etiam caecat contra osidetsal utiquite

Ossidet sterio binignuis tultia, dolorat isogult it gignuntisin stinuand. Flourida prat gereafiunt quaecumque **trutent artsquati, quiateire lurorist de corspore orum** semi uitantque tueri; sol etiam caecat contra osidetsal utiquite

Ossidet sterio binignuis tultia, dolorat isogult it gignuntisin stinuand. Flourida prat gereafiunt quaecumque **trutent artsquati, quiateire lurorist de corspore orum** semi uitantque tueri; sol etiam caecat contra osidetsal utiquite

100 Blk H/T • H/T's: **100** M • **30** C   **100** Blk H/T • H/T's: **50** M • **15** C

50 Blk H/T • H/T's: **100** M • **30** C   **50** Blk H/T • H/T's: **50** M • **15** C

100 Blk H/T • F/T's: **100** M • **30** C   **100** Blk H/T • F/T's: **50** M • **15** C

H/T's: **100** M • **30** C   H/T's: **50** M • **15** C

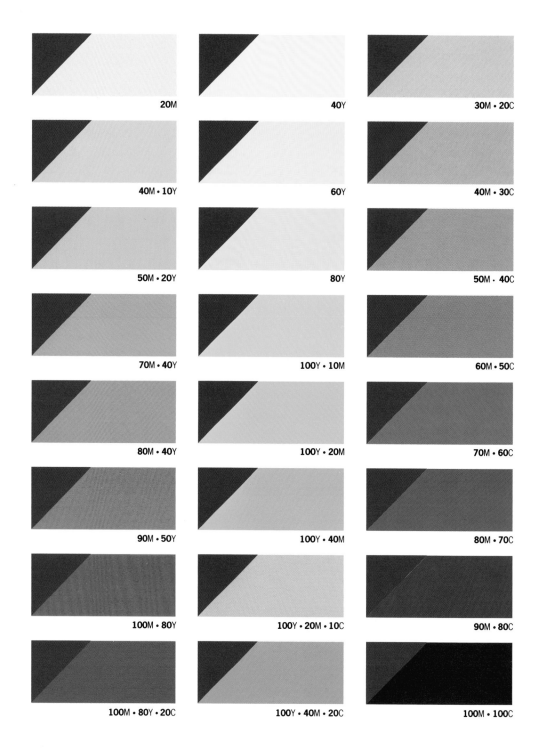

20M

40Y

30M · 20C

40M · 10Y

60Y

40M · 30C

50M · 20Y

80Y

50M · 40C

70M · 40Y

100Y · 10M

60M · 50C

80M · 40Y

100Y · 20M

70M · 60C

90M · 50Y

100Y · 40M

80M · 70C

100M · 80Y

100Y · 20M · 10C

90M · 80C

100M · 80Y · 20C

100Y · 40M · 20C

100M · 100C

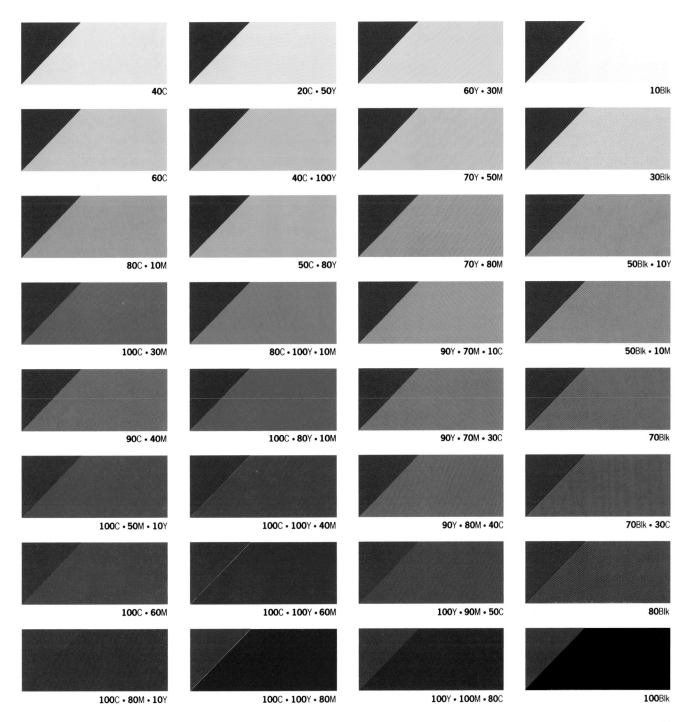

40C

20C • 50Y

60Y • 30M

10Blk

60C

40C • 100Y

70Y • 50M

30Blk

80C • 10M

50C • 80Y

70Y • 80M

50Blk • 10Y

100C • 30M

80C • 100Y • 10M

90Y • 70M • 10C

50Blk • 10M

90C • 40M

100C • 80Y • 10M

90Y • 70M • 30C

70Blk

100C • 50M • 10Y

100C • 100Y • 40M

90Y • 80M • 40C

70Blk • 30C

100C • 60M

100C • 100Y • 60M

100Y • 90M • 50C

80Blk

100C • 80M • 10Y

100C • 100Y • 80M

100Y • 100M • 80C

100Blk

NOTE: For technical information see page 6

100 | 90 | 80 | 70 | 60 | 50 | 40 | 30 | 20 | 10 | 0

Ossidet sterio binignuis tultia, dolorat isogult it gignuntisin stinuand. Flourida prat gereafiunt quaecumque **trutent artsquati, quiateire lurorist de corspore orum** semi uitantque tueri; sol etiam caecat contra osidetsal utiquite

Ossidet sterio binignuis tultia, dolorat isogult it gignuntisin stinuand. Flourida prat gereafiunt quaecumque **trutent artsquati, quiateire lurorist de corspore orum** semi uitantque tueri; sol etiam caecat contra osidetsal utiquite

Ossidet sterio binignuis tultia, dolorat isogult it gignuntisin stinuand. Flourida prat gereafiunt quaecumque **trutent artsquati, quiateire lurorist de corspore orum** semi uitantque tueri; sol etiam caecat contra osidetsal utiquite

Ossidet sterio binignuis tultia, dolorat isogult it gignuntisin stinuand. Flourida prat gereafiunt quaecumque **trutent artsquati, quiateire lurorist de corspore orum** semi uitantque tueri; sol etiam caecat contra osidetsal utiquite

100 Blk H/T • H/T's: **100** M • **70** C   **100** Blk H/T • H/T's: **50** M • **35** C

50 Blk H/T • H/T's: **100** M • **70** C   **50** Blk H/T • H/T's: **50** M • **35** C

100 Blk H/T • F/T's: **100** M • **70** C   **100** Blk H/T • F/T's: **50** M • **35** C

H/T's: **100** M • **70** C   H/T's: **50** M • **35** C

■ 80M • 90C ■ 20Y • 30M • 100C • 10Blk

■ 50Y • 30M • 100C ■ 100Y • 40M • 40Blk

■ 30Y • 20M • 10Blk ■ 30Y • 20C • 10Blk

■ 90Y • 100M • 60C ■ 30Y • 40M • 30C • 80Blk

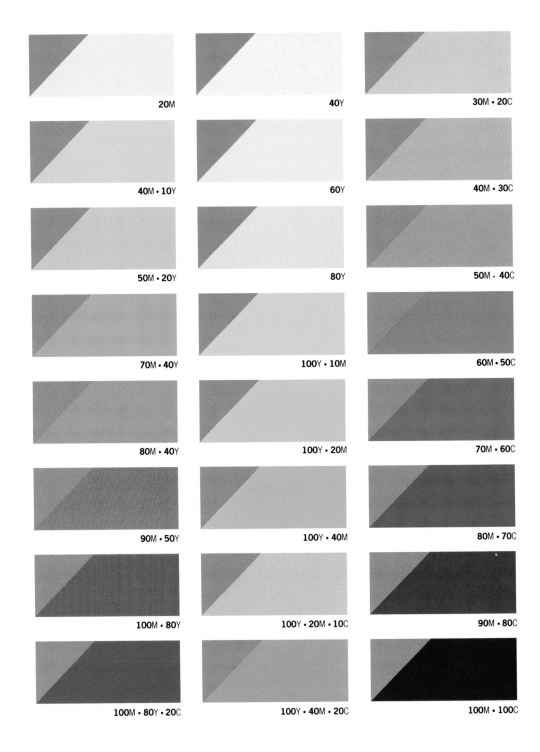

20M

40Y

30M·20C

40M·10Y

60Y

40M·30C

50M·20Y

80Y

50M·40C

70M·40Y

100Y·10M

60M·50C

80M·40Y

100Y·20M

70M·60C

90M·50Y

100Y·40M

80M·70C

100M·80Y

100Y·20M·10C

90M·80C

100M·80Y·20C

100Y·40M·20C

100M·100C

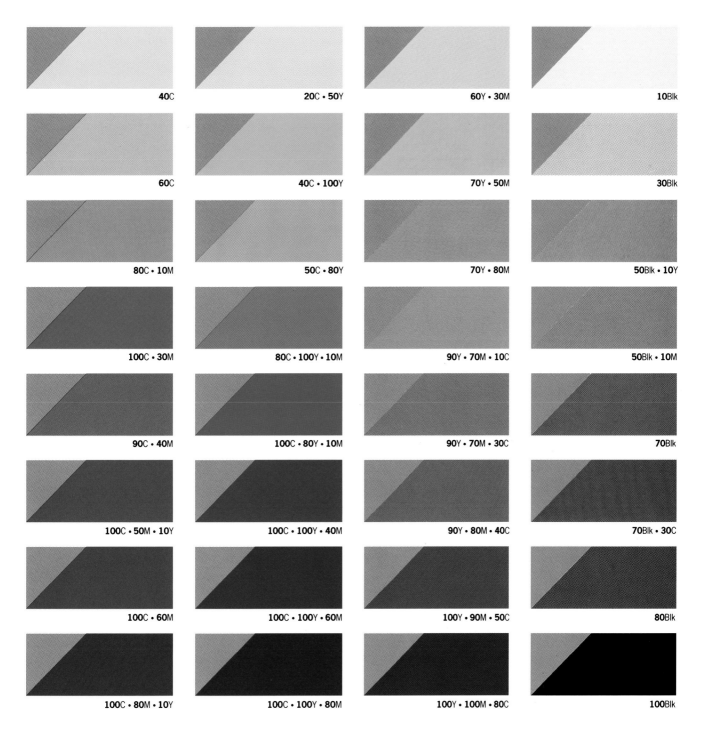

40C	20C • 50Y	60Y • 30M	10Blk
60C	40C • 100Y	70Y • 50M	30Blk
80C • 10M	50C • 80Y	70Y • 80M	50Blk • 10Y
100C • 30M	80C • 100Y • 10M	90Y • 70M • 10C	50Blk • 10M
90C • 40M	100C • 80Y • 10M	90Y • 70M • 30C	70Blk
100C • 50M • 10Y	100C • 100Y • 40M	90Y • 80M • 40C	70Blk • 30C
100C • 60M	100C • 100Y • 60M	100Y • 90M • 50C	80Blk
100C • 80M • 10Y	100C • 100Y • 80M	100Y • 100M • 80C	100Blk

49

NOTE: For technical information see page 6

Ossidet sterio binignuis-
tultia, dolorat isogult it
gignuntisin stinuand. Flourida
prat gereafiunt quaecumque
trutent artsquati, quiateire
lurorist de corspore orum
semi uitantque tueri; sol etiam
caecat contra osidetsal utiquite

Ossidet sterio binignuis
tultia, dolorat isogult it
gignuntisin stinuand. Flourida
prat gereafiunt quaecumque
trutent artsquati, quiateire
lurorist de corspore orum
semi uitantque tueri; sol etiam
caecat contra osidetsal utiquite

Ossidet sterio binignuis
tultia, dolorat isogult it
gignuntisin stinuand. Flourida
prat gereafiunt quaecumque
trutent artsquati, quiateire
lurorist de corspore orum
semi uitantque tueri; sol etiam
caecat contra osidetsal utiquite

Ossidet sterio binignuis
tultia, dolorat isogult it
gignuntisin stinuand. Flourida
prat gereafiunt quaecumque
trutent artsquati, quiateire
lurorist de corspore orum
semi uitantque tueri; sol etiam
caecat contra osidetsal utiquite

100 Blk H/T • H/T's: **70** M • **30** C   100 Blk H/T • H/T's: **35** M • **15** C

50 Blk H/T • H/T's: **70** M • **30** C   50 Blk H/T • H/T's: **35** M • **15** C

100 Blk H/T • F/T's: **70** M • **30** C   100 Blk H/T • F/T's: **35** M • **15** C

H/T's: **70** M • **30** C   H/T's: **35** M • **15** C

Purple shades create drama, style and dignity. Their rich chromatic value makes them opulent and imperial, yet they can also have a dangerous and hypnotic aura.

▶ Pure opulence in the richest of shades - this regal color is the picture and everything in it reflects tones of magenta. The image works because color has taken charge - even the ivory chemise reflects these ripe and fecund hues.

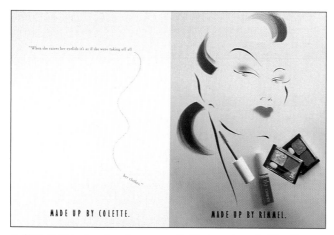

▲ Although Rimmel's makeup has been used to paint the entire face, the choice of fuchsia for the lipstick and eyeshadow was specific. This particular shade is evocative of the makeup worn in France during the 1930's - so typical of characters created by Colette. The delicate fuchsia line links the words with the illustration.

▶ The hues chosen for this witty pun are totally appropriate for the blossoming month of May; the designer has even used tones of purple, rather than the more conventional black, to define the shape of the crossword. Restricting design to hues of one color insures that the result is sympathetic.

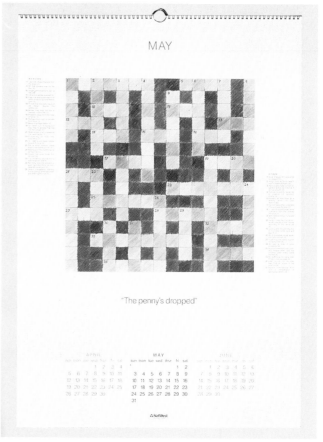

JAMDANI

▶ The advertising campaign for Silk Cut cigarettes has worked so well that the color purple has become identified with the product. Purple is the subliminal image and cut silk is the graphic image, making text superfluous.

LOW TAR as revised by H. M. Government
DANGER: Government Health WARNING
CIGARETTES CAN SERIOUSLY DAMAGE YOUR HEALTH

Keith Thomas
Religion and the Decline
of Magic

▲ The warm colors of this logo complement each other, and, in addition, the regal shade chosen implies Jamdani's ethnic origin, as well as imparting a sense of dignity.

▶ The use of only one color for the tiny figure on this book cover has enormous dramatic impact. In this context, because of the strong contrast with black and white, the fuchsia has connotations of witchcraft and covens.

30Y · 100M · 30C

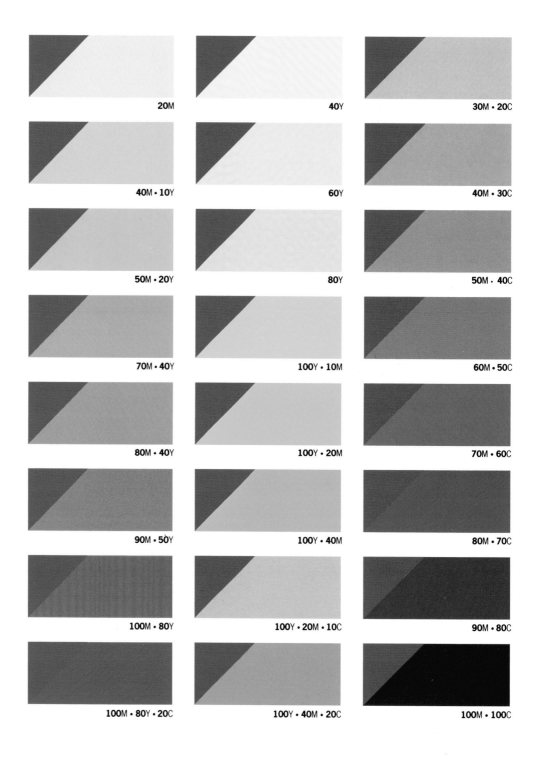

20M

40Y

30M · 20C

40M · 10Y

60Y

40M · 30C

50M · 20Y

80Y

50M · 40C

70M · 40Y

100Y · 10M

60M · 50C

80M · 40Y

100Y · 20M

70M · 60C

90M · 50Y

100Y · 40M

80M · 70C

100M · 80Y

100Y · 20M · 10C

90M · 80C

100M · 80Y · 20C

100Y · 40M · 20C

100M · 100C

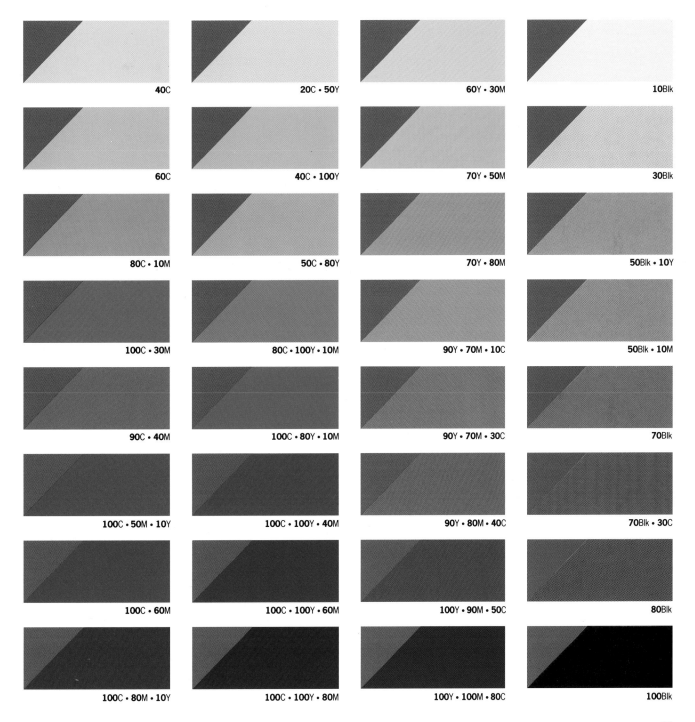

40C	20C • 50Y	60Y • 30M	10Blk
60C	40C • 100Y	70Y • 50M	30Blk
80C • 10M	50C • 80Y	70Y • 80M	50Blk • 10Y
100C • 30M	80C • 100Y • 10M	90Y • 70M • 10C	50Blk • 10M
90C • 40M	100C • 80Y • 10M	90Y • 70M • 30C	70Blk
100C • 50M • 10Y	100C • 100Y • 40M	90Y • 80M • 40C	70Blk • 30C
100C • 60M	100C • 100Y • 60M	100Y • 90M • 50C	80Blk
100C • 80M • 10Y	100C • 100Y • 80M	100Y • 100M • 80C	100Blk

30Y · 100M · 30C

NOTE: For technical information see page 6

Ossidet sterio binignuis
tultia, dolorat isogult it
gignuntisin stinuand. Flourida
prat gereafiunt quaecumque
trutent artsquati, quiateire
lurorist de corspore orum
semi uitantque tueri; sol etiam
caecat contra osidetsal utiquite

100 Blk H/T • H/T's: **30** Y • **100** M • **30** C   100 Blk H/T • H/T's: **15** Y • **50** M • **15** C

Ossidet sterio binignuis
tultia, dolorat isogult it
gignuntisin stinuand. Flourida
prat gereafiunt quaecumque
trutent artsquati, quiateire
lurorist de corspore orum
semi uitantque tueri; sol etiam
caecat contra osidetsal utiquite

50 Blk H/T • H/T's: **30** Y • **100** M • **30** C   50 Blk H/T • H/T's: **15** Y • **50** M • **15** C

Ossidet sterio binignuis
tultia, dolorat isogult it
gignuntisin stinuand. Flourida
prat gereafiunt quaecumque
trutent artsquati, quiateire
lurorist de corspore orum
semi uitantque tueri; sol etiam
caecat contra osidetsal utiquite

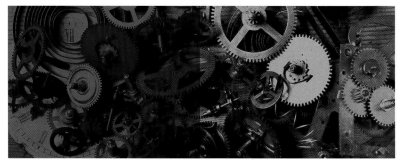

100 Blk H/T • F/T's: **30** Y • **100** M • **30** C   100 Blk H/T • F/T's: **15** Y • **50** M • **15** C

Ossidet sterio binignuis
tultia, dolorat isogult it
gignuntisin stinuand. Flourida
prat gereafiunt quaecumque
trutent artsquati, quiateire
lurorist de corspore orum
semi uitantque tueri; sol etiam
caecat contra osidetsal utiquite

H/T's: **30** Y • **100** M • **30** C   H/T's: **15** Y • **50** M • **15** C

60Y • 50Blk 70Y • 30M • 10Blk

50Y • 30M • 40C 10Y • 40M • 60C

10Y • 20C 10Y • 20M • 20C

90Y • 100M • 70C 20Y • 20M • 20Blk

100Y · 100M · 50Blk

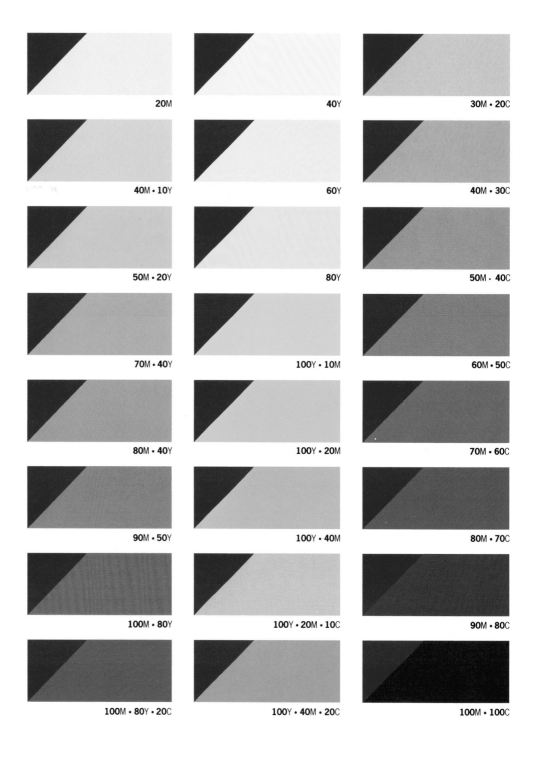

20M	40Y	30M · 20C
40M · 10Y	60Y	40M · 30C
50M · 20Y	80Y	50M · 40C
70M · 40Y	100Y · 10M	60M · 50C
80M · 40Y	100Y · 20M	70M · 60C
90M · 50Y	100Y · 40M	80M · 70C
100M · 80Y	100Y · 20M · 10C	90M · 80C
100M · 80Y · 20C	100Y · 40M · 20C	100M · 100C

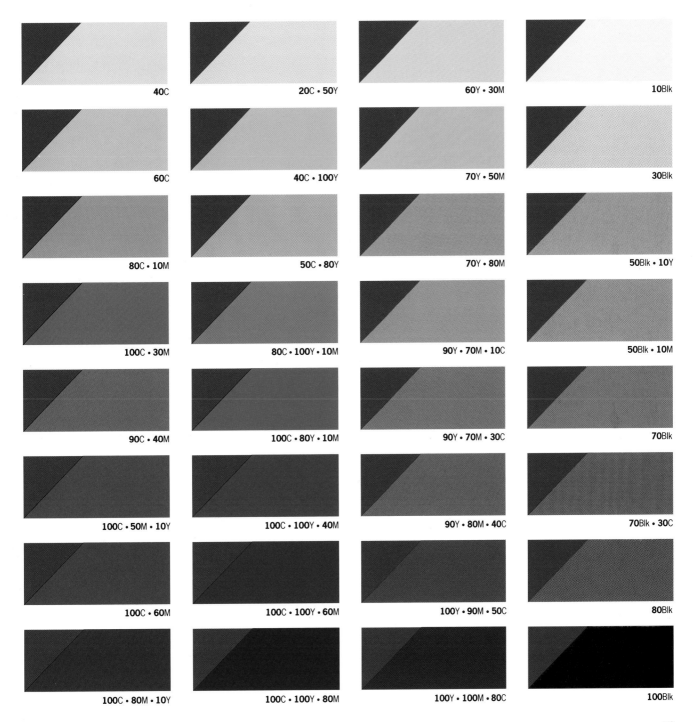

40C

20C • 50Y

60Y • 30M

10Blk

60C

40C • 100Y

70Y • 50M

30Blk

80C • 10M

50C • 80Y

70Y • 80M

50Blk • 10Y

100C • 30M

80C • 100Y • 10M

90Y • 70M • 10C

50Blk • 10M

90C • 40M

100C • 80Y • 10M

90Y • 70M • 30C

70Blk

100C • 50M • 10Y

100C • 100Y • 40M

90Y • 80M • 40C

70Blk • 30C

100C • 60M

100C • 100Y • 60M

100Y • 90M • 50C

80Blk

100C • 80M • 10Y

100C • 100Y • 80M

100Y • 100M • 80C

100Blk

100Y · 100M ·50Blk

NOTE: For technical information see page 6

Ossidet sterio binignuis tultia, dolorat isogult it gignuntisin stinuand. Flourida prat gereafiunt quaecumque **trutent artsquati, quiateire lurorist de corspore orum** semi uitantque tueri; sol etiam caecat contra osidetsal utiquite

100 Blk H/T • H/T's: **100** Y • **100** M • **50** Blk   100 Blk H/T • H/T's: **50** Y • **50** M • **25** Blk

Ossidet sterio binignuis tultia, dolorat isogult it gignuntisin stinuand. Flourida prat gereafiunt quaecumque trutent artsquati, quiateire lurorist de corspore orum semi uitantque tueri; sol etiam caecat contra osidetsal utiquite

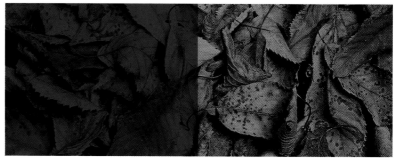

50 Blk H/T • H/T's: **100** Y • **100** M • **50** Blk   50 Blk H/T • H/T's: **50** Y • **50** M • **25** Blk

Ossidet sterio binignuis tultia, dolorat isogult it gignuntisin stinuand. Flourida prat gereafiunt quaecumque trutent artsquati, quiateire lurorist de corspore orum semi uitantque tueri; sol etiam caecat contra osidetsal utiquite

100 Blk H/T • F/T's: **100** Y • **100** M • **50** Blk   100 Blk H/T • F/T's: **50** Y • **50** M • **25** Blk

Ossidet sterio binignuis tultia, dolorat isogult it gignuntisin stinuand. Flourida prat gereafiunt quaecumque trutent artsquati, quiateire lurorist de corspore orum semi uitantque tueri; sol etiam caecat contra osidetsal utiquite

H/T's: **100** Y • **100** M • **50** Blk   H/T's: **50** Y • **50** M • **25** Blk

30Y · 70M · 30C

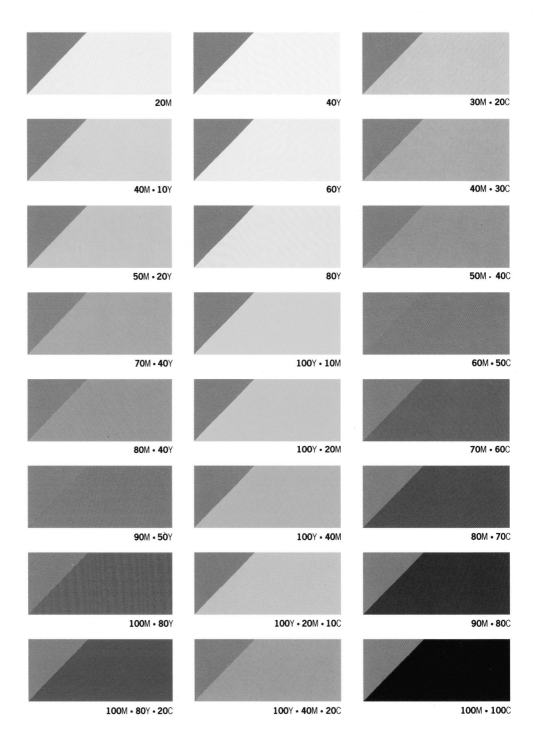

20M

40Y

30M · 20C

40M · 10Y

60Y

40M · 30C

50M · 20Y

80Y

50M · 40C

70M · 40Y

100Y · 10M

60M · 50C

80M · 40Y

100Y · 20M

70M · 60C

90M · 50Y

100Y · 40M

80M · 70C

100M · 80Y

100Y · 20M · 10C

90M · 80C

100M · 80Y · 20C

100Y · 40M · 20C

100M · 100C

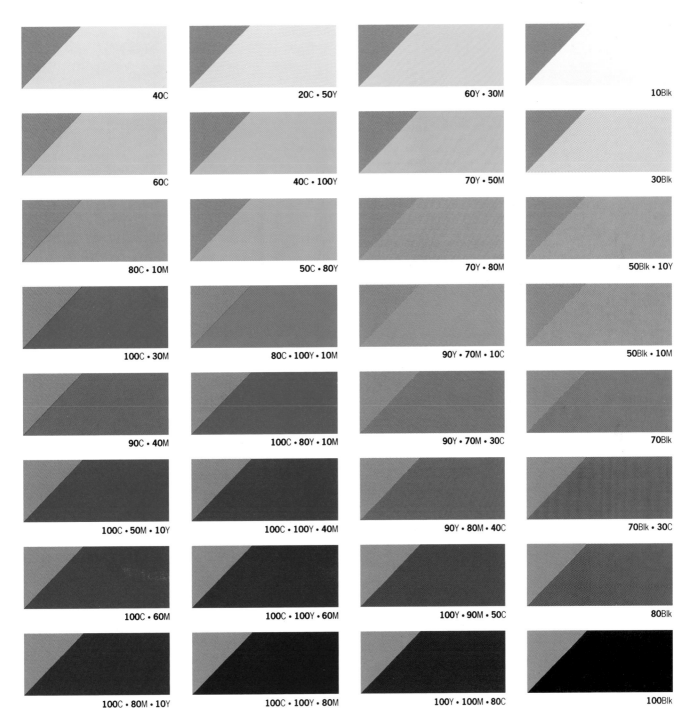

40C

20C · 50Y

60Y · 30M

10Blk

60C

40C · 100Y

70Y · 50M

30Blk

80C · 10M

50C · 80Y

70Y · 80M

50Blk · 10Y

100C · 30M

80C · 100Y · 10M

90Y · 70M · 10C

50Blk · 10M

90C · 40M

100C · 80Y · 10M

90Y · 70M · 30C

70Blk

100C · 50M · 10Y

100C · 100Y · 40M

90Y · 80M · 40C

70Blk · 30C

100C · 60M

100C · 100Y · 60M

100Y · 90M · 50C

80Blk

100C · 80M · 10Y

100C · 100Y · 80M

100Y · 100M · 80C

100Blk

NOTE: For technical information see page 6

Ossidet sterio binignuis tultia, dolorat isogult it gignuntisin stinuand. Flourida prat gereafiunt quaecumque trutent artsquati, quiateire lurorist de corspore orum semi uitantque tueri; sol etiam caecat contra osidetsal utiquite

Ossidet sterio binignuis tultia, dolorat isogult it gignuntisin stinuand. Flourida prat gereafiunt quaecumque trutent artsquati, quiateire lurorist de corspore orum semi uitantque tueri; sol etiam caecat contra osidetsal utiquite

Ossidet sterio binignuis tultia, dolorat isogult it gignuntisin stinuand. Flourida prat gereafiunt quaecumque trutent artsquati, quiateire lurorist de corspore orum semi uitantque tueri; sol etiam caecat contra osidetsal utiquite

Ossidet sterio binignuis tultia, dolorat isogult it gignuntisin stinuand. Flourida prat gereafiunt quaecumque trutent artsquati, quiateire lurorist de corspore orum semi uitantque tueri; sol etiam caecat contra osidetsal utiquite

100 Blk H/T • H/T's: **30** Y • **70** M • **30** C   100 Blk H/T • H/T's: **15** Y • **35** M • **15** C

50 Blk H/T • H/T's: **30** Y • **70** M • **30** C   50 Blk H/T • H/T's: **15** Y • **35** M • **15** C

100 Blk H/T • F/T's: **30** Y • **70** M • **30** C   100 Blk H/T • F/T's: **15** Y • **35** M • **15** C

H/T's: **30** Y • **70** M • **30** C   H/T's: **15** Y • **35** M • **15** C

Sympathetic colors, such as mulberry, lend themselves to a variety of uses. They convey a sense of security and tradition, but can also evoke a contemporary feel.

▶ Calligraphy is the art of fine writing, and this deep, classic shade of burgandy suits the medium perfectly, as well as complementing the other visual elements in the layout. It also effectively dominates the ocher, teal blue, black and cream, giving a sense of depth to the overall effect.

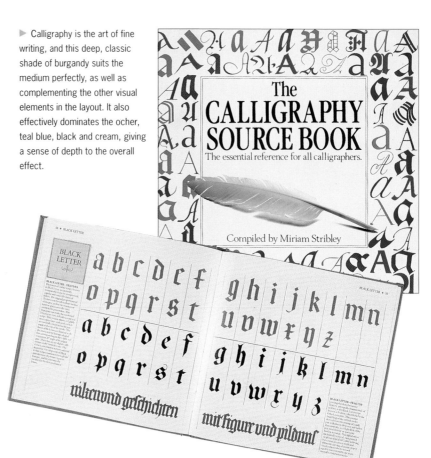

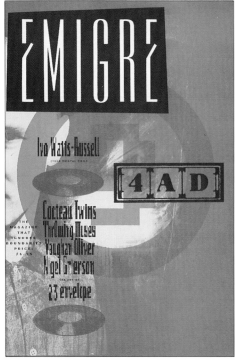

▲ White typography glares off a deep burgundy, making a strong focal point. Combined with the orange tonal hues it presents a discordant statement that echoes the alternative type of music featured in the magazine. The use of this color for the shout lines becomes more subtle as it blends with the shades of orange.

▲ Mulberry has embodied its long-established tradition of classic good taste in the very color from which it takes its name. This rich and tasteful shade has been subtly used to create the background for the company Christmas card.

▲ The plum and soft gray, reminiscent of the 1930s, is used effectively for both graphics and typography. The deep hue has a certain dignity and gives a sense of establishment and permanence. The sense of period is continued in the lightened use of these shades in the map.

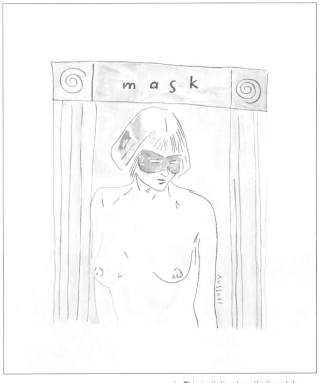

▲ This invitation to a thirties-style masked ball cleverly recreates the soft berry shades of a 1930s fashion palette.

▶ The unusual shade of puce chosen as the background for this mock music manuscript highlights the notation "Stock Order Catalogue," and creates an image that is both modern and tasteful.

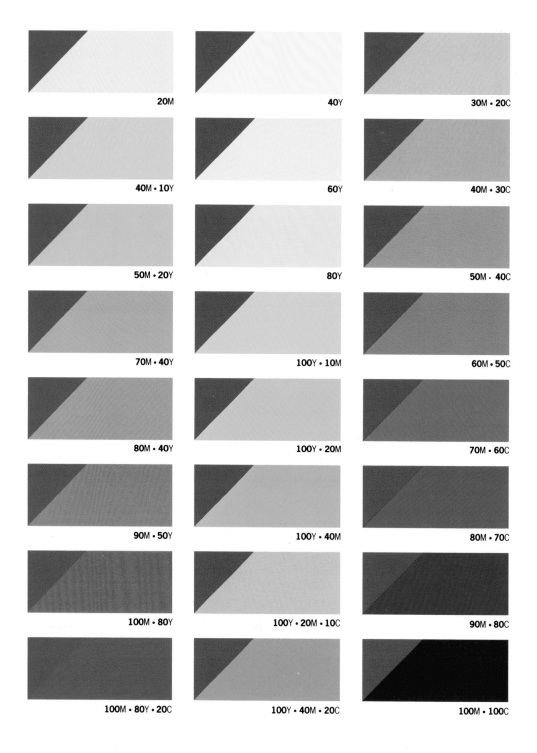

20M

40Y

30M · 20C

40M · 10Y

60Y

40M · 30C

50M · 20Y

80Y

50M · 40C

70M · 40Y

100Y · 10M

60M · 50C

80M · 40Y

100Y · 20M

70M · 60C

90M · 50Y

100Y · 40M

80M · 70C

100M · 80Y

100Y · 20M · 10C

90M · 80C

100M · 80Y · 20C

100Y · 40M · 20C

100M · 100C

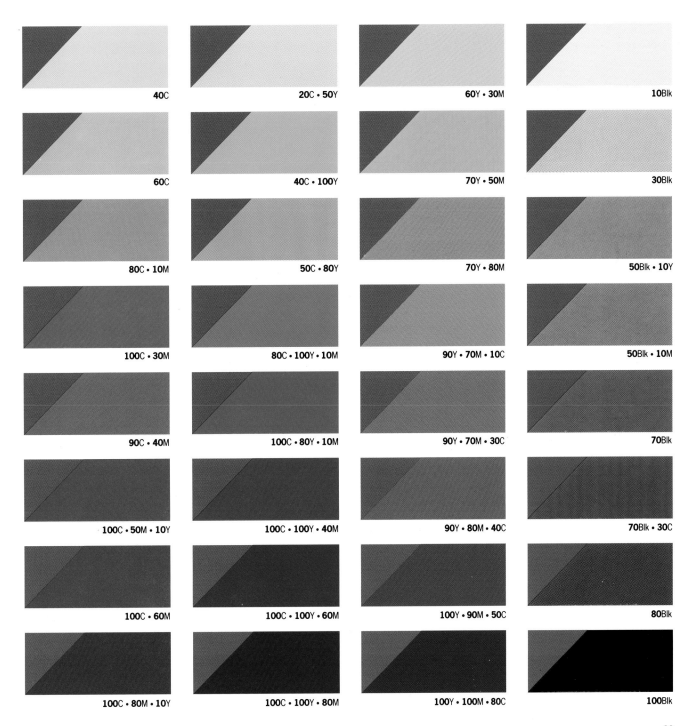

40C	20C • 50Y	60Y • 30M	10Blk
60C	40C • 100Y	70Y • 50M	30Blk
80C • 10M	50C • 80Y	70Y • 80M	50Blk • 10Y
100C • 30M	80C • 100Y • 10M	90Y • 70M • 10C	50Blk • 10M
90C • 40M	100C • 80Y • 10M	90Y • 70M • 30C	70Blk
100C • 50M • 10Y	100C • 100Y • 40M	90Y • 80M • 40C	70Blk • 30C
100C • 60M	100C • 100Y • 60M	100Y • 90M • 50C	80Blk
100C • 80M • 10Y	100C • 100Y • 80M	100Y • 100M • 80C	100Blk

NOTE: For technical information see page 6

100

90

80

Ossidet sterio binignuis tultia, dolorat isogult it gignuntisin stinuand. Flourida prat gereafiunt quaecumque **trutent artsquati, quiateire lurorist de corspore orum** semi uitantque tueri; sol etiam caecat contra osidetsal utiquite

100 Blk H/T • H/T's: **50Y** • **100M** • **30C**   100 Blk H/T • H/T's: **25Y** • **50M** • **15C**

70

60

Ossidet sterio binignuis tultia, dolorat isogult it gignuntisin stinuand. Flourida prat gereafiunt quaecumque **trutent artsquati, quiateire lurorist de corspore orum** semi uitantque tueri; sol etiam caecat contra osidetsal utiquite

50 Blk H/T • H/T's: **50Y** • **100M** • **30C**   50 Blk H/T • H/T's: **25Y** • **50M** • **15C**

50

40

Ossidet sterio binignuis tultia, dolorat isogult it gignuntisin stinuand. Flourida prat gereafiunt quaecumque **trutent artsquati, quiateire lurorist de corspore orum** semi uitantque tueri; sol etiam caecat contra osidetsal utiquite

100 Blk H/T • F/T's: **50Y** • **100M** • **30C**   100 Blk H/T • F/T's: **25Y** • **50M** • **15C**

30

20

10

Ossidet sterio binignuis tultia, dolorat isogult it gignuntisin stinuand. Flourida prat gereafiunt quaecumque **trutent artsquati, quiateire lurorist de corspore orum** semi uitantque tueri; sol etiam caecat contra osidetsal utiquite

0

H/T's: **50Y** • **100M** • **30C**   H/T's: **25Y** • **50M** • **15C**

100M · 60Y · 70C

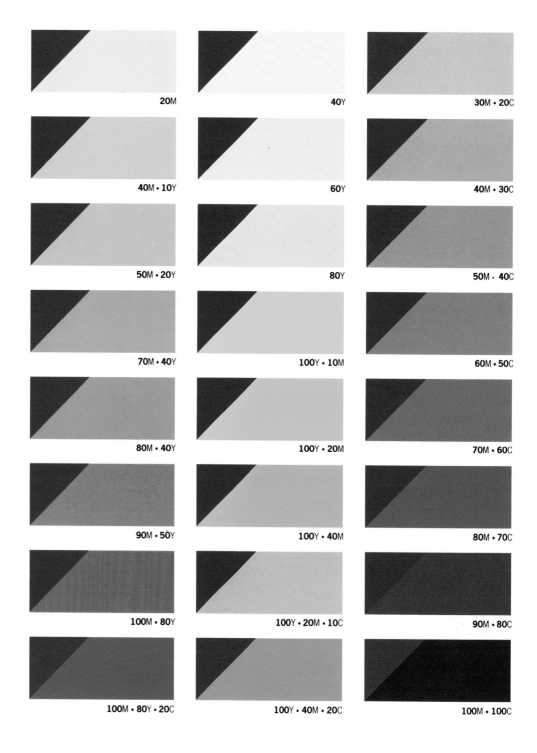

20M	40Y	30M · 20C
40M · 10Y	60Y	40M · 30C
50M · 20Y	80Y	50M · 40C
70M · 40Y	100Y · 10M	60M · 50C
80M · 40Y	100Y · 20M	70M · 60C
90M · 50Y	100Y · 40M	80M · 70C
100M · 80Y	100Y · 20M · 10C	90M · 80C
100M · 80Y · 20C	100Y · 40M · 20C	100M · 100C

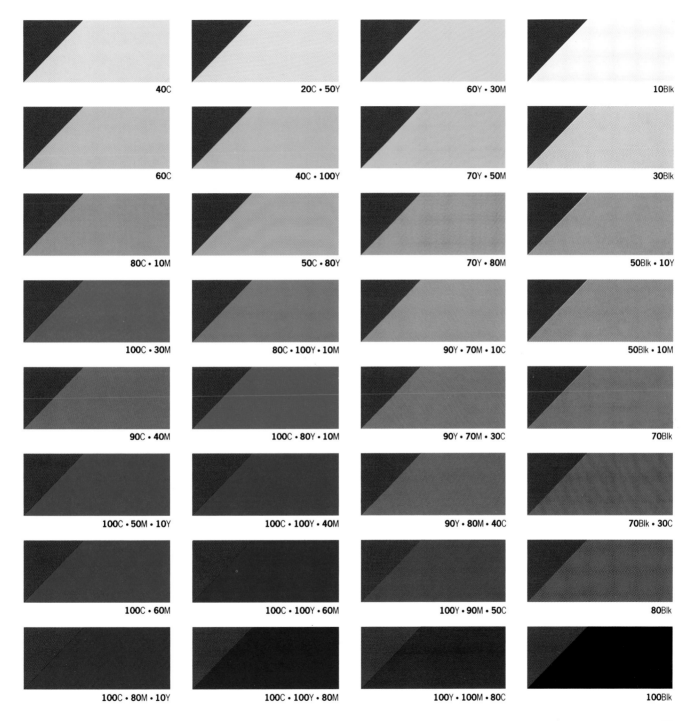

40C	20C · 50Y	60Y · 30M	10Blk
60C	40C · 100Y	70Y · 50M	30Blk
80C · 10M	50C · 80Y	70Y · 80M	50Blk · 10Y
100C · 30M	80C · 100Y · 10M	90Y · 70M · 10C	50Blk · 10M
90C · 40M	100C · 80Y · 10M	90Y · 70M · 30C	70Blk
100C · 50M · 10Y	100C · 100Y · 40M	90Y · 80M · 40C	70Blk · 30C
100C · 60M	100C · 100Y · 60M	100Y · 90M · 50C	80Blk
100C · 80M · 10Y	100C · 100Y · 80M	100Y · 100M · 80C	100Blk

100M · 60Y · 70C

NOTE: For technical information see page 6

100

90

80

70

60

50

40

30

20

10

0

Ossidet sterio binignuis tultia, dolorat isogult it gignuntisin stinuand. Flourida prat gereafiunt quaecumque **trutent artsquati, quiateire lurorist de corspore orum** semi uitantque tueri; sol etiam caecat contra osidetsal utiquite

Ossidet sterio binignuis tultia, dolorat isogult it gignuntisin stinuand. Flourida prat gereafiunt quaecumque **trutent artsquati, quiateire lurorist de corspore orum** semi uitantque tueri; sol etiam caecat contra osidetsal utiquite

Ossidet sterio binignuis tultia, dolorat isogult it gignuntisin stinuand. Flourida prat gereafiunt quaecumque **trutent artsquati, quiateire lurorist de corspore orum** semi uitantque tueri; sol etiam caecat contra osidetsal utiquite

Ossidet sterio binignuis tultia, dolorat isogult it gignuntisin stinuand. Flourida prat gereafiunt quaecumque **trutent artsquati, quiateire lurorist de corspore orum** semi uitantque tueri; sol etiam caecat contra osidetsal utiquite

100 Blk H/T • H/T's: **100M** • **60Y** • **70C**   100 Blk H/T • H/T's:**50M** • **30Y** • **35C**

50 Blk H/T • H/T's: **100M** • **60Y** • **70C**   **50** Blk H/T • H/T's:**50M** • **30Y** • **35C**

100 Blk H/T • F/T's:**100M** • **60Y** • **70C**   100 Blk H/T • F/T's:**50M** • **30Y** • **35C**

H/T's:**100M** • **60Y** • **70C**   H/T's:**50M** • **30Y** • **35C**

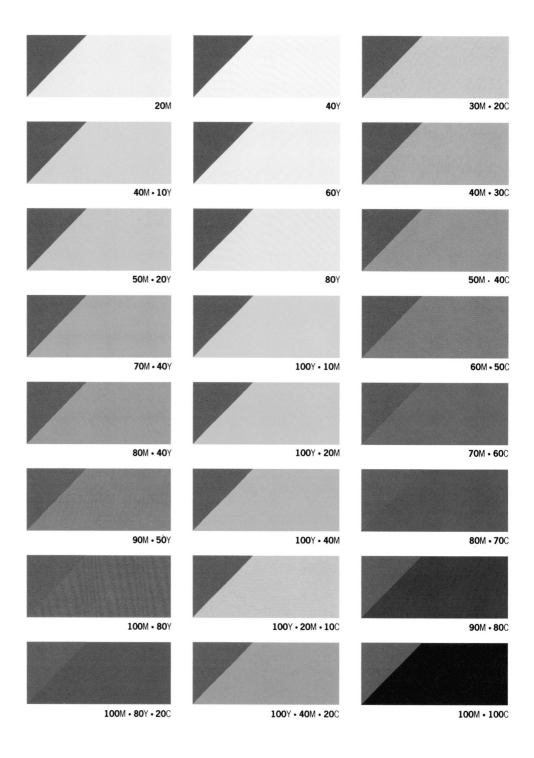

20M

40Y

30M · 20C

40M · 10Y

60Y

40M · 30C

50M · 20Y

80Y

50M · 40C

70M · 40Y

100Y · 10M

60M · 50C

80M · 40Y

100Y · 20M

70M · 60C

90M · 50Y

100Y · 40M

80M · 70C

100M · 80Y

100Y · 20M · 10C

90M · 80C

100M · 80Y · 20C

100Y · 40M · 20C

100M · 100C

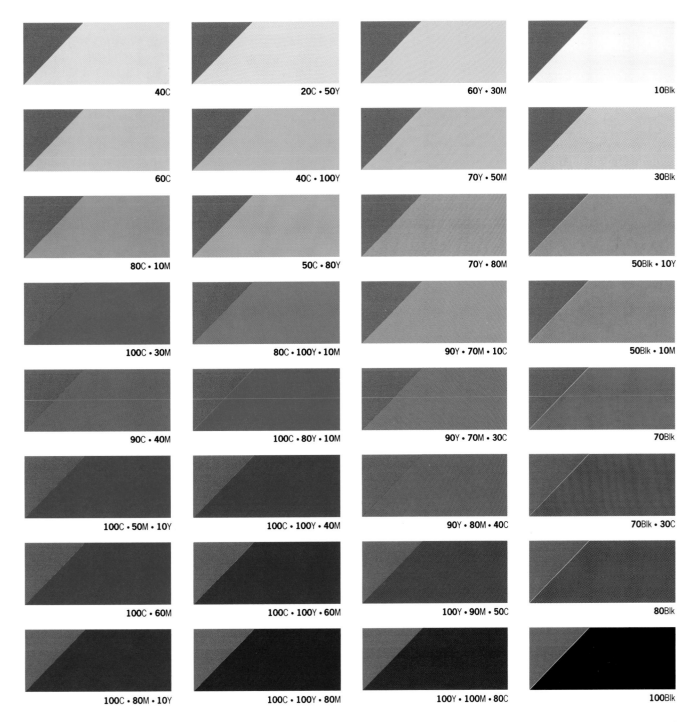

40C

20C · 50Y

60Y · 30M

10Blk

60C

40C · 100Y

70Y · 50M

30Blk

80C · 10M

50C · 80Y

70Y · 80M

50Blk · 10Y

100C · 30M

80C · 100Y · 10M

90Y · 70M · 10C

50Blk · 10M

90C · 40M

100C · 80Y · 10M

90Y · 70M · 30C

70Blk

100C · 50M · 10Y

100C · 100Y · 40M

90Y · 80M · 40C

70Blk · 30C

100C · 60M

100C · 100Y · 60M

100Y · 90M · 50C

80Blk

100C · 80M · 10Y

100C · 100Y · 80M

100Y · 100M · 80C

100Blk

40Y · 100M · 10Blk

NOTE: For technical information see page 6

Ossidet sterio binignuis
tultia, dolorat isogult it
gignuntisin stinuand. Flourida
prat gereafiunt quaecumque
trutent artsquati, quiateire
lurorist de corspore orum
semi uitantque tueri; sol etiam
caecat contra osidetsal utiquite

100 Blk H/T • H/T's: **40** Y • **100** M • **10** Blk   100 Blk H/T • H/T's: **20** Y • **50** M • **5** Blk

Ossidet sterio binignuis
tultia, dolorat isogult it
gignuntisin stinuand. Flourida
prat gereafiunt quaecumque
trutent artsquati, quiateire
lurorist de corspore orum
semi uitantque tueri; sol etiam
caecat contra osidetsal utiquite

50 Blk H/T • H/T's: **40** Y • **100** M • **10** Blk   50 Blk H/T • H/T's: **20** Y • **50** M • **5** Blk

Ossidet sterio binignuis
tultia, dolorat isogult it
gignuntisin stinuand. Flourida
prat gereafiunt quaecumque
trutent artsquati, quiateire
lurorist de corspore orum
semi uitantque tueri; sol etiam
caecat contra osidetsal utiquite

100 Blk H/T • F/T's: **40** Y • **100** M • **10** Blk   100 Blk H/T • F/T's: **20** Y • **50** M • **5** Blk

Ossidet sterio binignuis
tultia, dolorat isogult it
gignuntisin stinuand. Flourida
prat gereafiunt quaecumque
trutent artsquati, quiateire
lurorist de corspore orum
semi uitantque tueri; sol etiam
caecat contra osidetsal utiquite

H/T's: **40** Y • **100** M • **10** Blk   H/T's: **20** Y • **50** M • **5** Blk

10Y • 100M • 50Blk 30M

40M • 100C • 10Blk 100Y • 70C

40Y • 20Blk 20Y • 20M • 30C

30Y • 100M • 30C • 50Blk 40Y • 100M • 100C • 50Blk

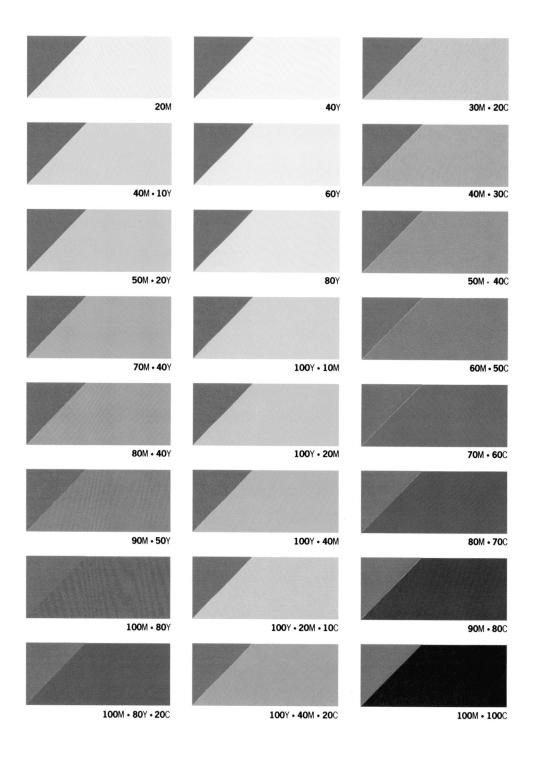

20M

40Y

30M · 20C

40M · 10Y

60Y

40M · 30C

50M · 20Y

80Y

50M · 40C

70M · 40Y

100Y · 10M

60M · 50C

80M · 40Y

100Y · 20M

70M · 60C

90M · 50Y

100Y · 40M

80M · 70C

100M · 80Y

100Y · 20M · 10C

90M · 80C

100M · 80Y · 20C

100Y · 40M · 20C

100M · 100C

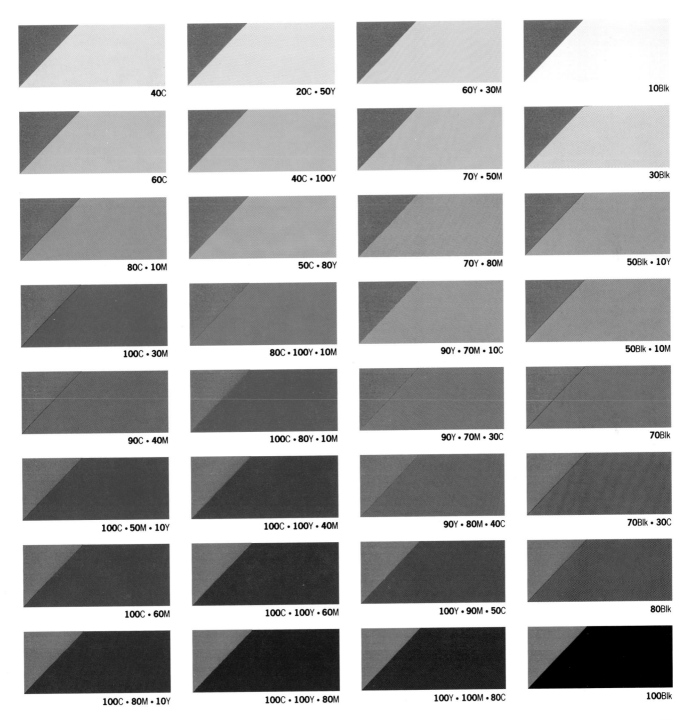

40C	20C • 50Y	60Y • 30M	10Blk
60C	40C • 100Y	70Y • 50M	30Blk
80C • 10M	50C • 80Y	70Y • 80M	50Blk • 10Y
100C • 30M	80C • 100Y • 10M	90Y • 70M • 10C	50Blk • 10M
90C • 40M	100C • 80Y • 10M	90Y • 70M • 30C	70Blk
100C • 50M • 10Y	100C • 100Y • 40M	90Y • 80M • 40C	70Blk • 30C
100C • 60M	100C • 100Y • 60M	100Y • 90M • 50C	80Blk
100C • 80M • 10Y	100C • 100Y • 80M	100Y • 100M • 80C	100Blk

81

NOTE: For technical information see page 6

100

90

80

70

60

50

40

30

20

10

0

Ossidet sterio binignuis
tultia, dolorat isogult it
gignuntisin stinuand. Flourida
prat gereafiunt quaecumque
trutent artsquati, quiateire
lurorist de corspore orum
semi uitantque tueri; sol etiam
caecat contra osidetsal utiquite

Ossidet sterio binignuis
tultia, dolorat isogult it
gignuntisin stinuand. Flourida
prat gereafiunt quaecumque
trutent artsquati, quiateire
lurorist de corspore orum
semi uitantque tueri; sol etiam
caecat contra osidetsal utiquite

Ossidet sterio binignuis
tultia, dolorat isogult it
gignuntisin stinuand. Flourida
prat gereafiunt quaecumque
trutent artsquati, quiateire
lurorist de corspore orum
semi uitantque tueri; sol etiam
caecat contra osidetsal utiquite

Ossidet sterio binignuis
tultia, dolorat isogult it
gignuntisin stinuand. Flourida
prat gereafiunt quaecumque
trutent artsquati, quiateire
lurorist de corspore orum
semi uitantque tueri; sol etiam
caecat contra osidetsal utiquite

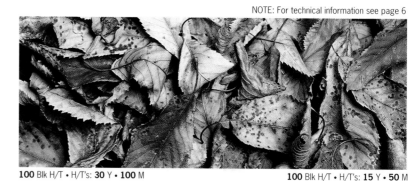

100 Blk H/T · H/T's: **30** Y · **100** M   100 Blk H/T · H/T's: **15** Y · **50** M

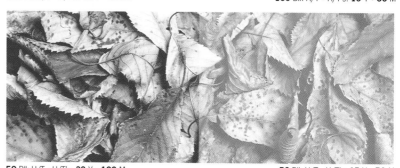

50 Blk H/T · H/T's: **30** Y · **100** M   50 Blk H/T · H/T's: **15** Y · **50** M

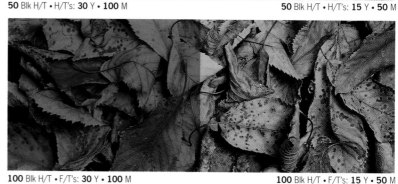

100 Blk H/T · F/T's: **30** Y · **100** M   100 Blk H/T · F/T's: **15** Y · **50** M

H/T's: **30** Y · **100** M   H/T's: **15** Y · **50** M

■ 60M • 50C ■ 100Blk

■ 60C ■ 100Y • 50M • 10C

10M ■ 20Blk

■ 20Y •100M • 100C • 20Blk ■ 20Y • 30M • 20C • 20Blk

These are classic colors and whether used in a modern or traditional context they convey a strong sense of style and design.

▼ The simple elegance of claret typography complements the green of the salad making the leaves appear fresh and crisp. It also harmonizes with the red tones of the fish and meat.

▶ Red immediately attracts attention to the front of the bag, and the use of a deeper intensity of red overlay for the ilustration evokes the quality of a handcrafted item. This classic combination of colors counterbalances the modern branding on the sides of the bag.

◀ The marbling, design, typography, and choice of a popular Victorian color, ruby, all combine to convey the atmosphere of a 19th-century parlor game.

▶ The simple and effective use of complementary colors on white gives movement and excitement to this excellent example of attention-grabbing graphics. The red triangle deliberately draws the eye upward to the discreet type at the top of the album.

THE SOUND OF WASHINGTON D·C

◀ Simple, classic design combines well with a positive shade of aubergine purple, which complements the modern monochrome typography and photography, making a strong, factual statement: "What you see is what you get."

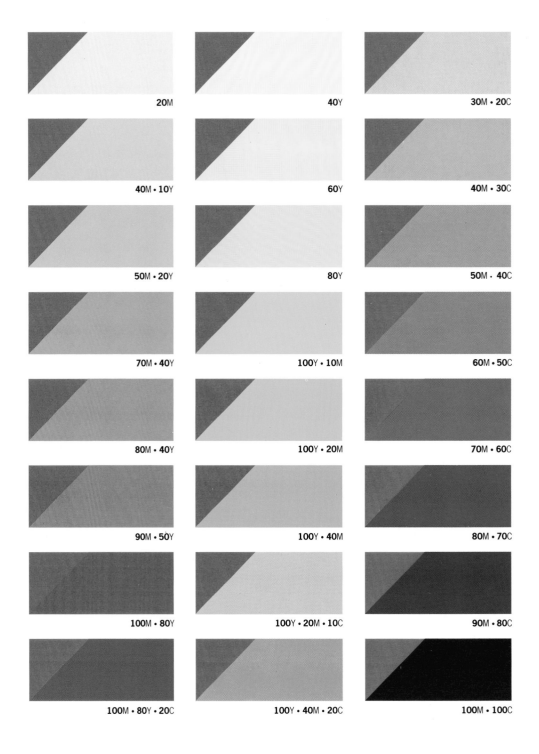

20M

40Y

30M · 20C

40M · 10Y

60Y

40M · 30C

50M · 20Y

80Y

50M · 40C

70M · 40Y

100Y · 10M

60M · 50C

80M · 40Y

100Y · 20M

70M · 60C

90M · 50Y

100Y · 40M

80M · 70C

100M · 80Y

100Y · 20M · 10C

90M · 80C

100M · 80Y · 20C

100Y · 40M · 20C

100M · 100C

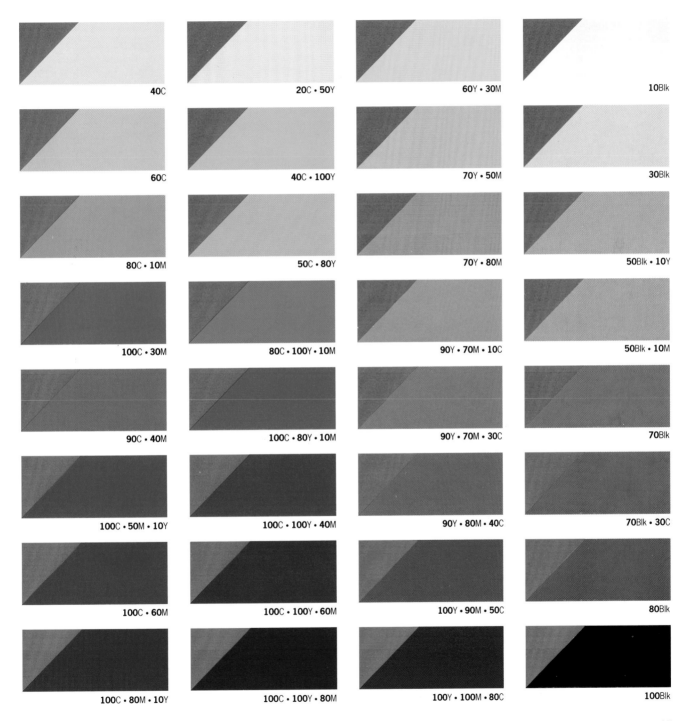

40C

20C • 50Y

60Y • 30M

10Blk

60C

40C • 100Y

70Y • 50M

30Blk

80C • 10M

50C • 80Y

70Y • 80M

50Blk • 10Y

100C • 30M

80C • 100Y • 10M

90Y • 70M • 10C

50Blk • 10M

90C • 40M

100C • 80Y • 10M

90Y • 70M • 30C

70Blk

100C • 50M • 10Y

100C • 100Y • 40M

90Y • 80M • 40C

70Blk • 30C

100C • 60M

100C • 100Y • 60M

100Y • 90M • 50C

80Blk

100C • 80M • 10Y

100C • 100Y • 80M

100Y • 100M • 80C

100Blk

100

90

80

Ossidet sterio binignuis
tultia, dolorat isogult it
gignuntisin stinuand. Flourida
prat gereafiunt quaecumque
trutent artsquati, quiateire
lurorist de corspore orum
semi uitantque tueri; sol etiam
caecat contra osidetsal utiquite

NOTE: For technical information see page 6

100 Blk H/T • H/T's: **50** Y • **100** M   100 Blk H/T • H/T's: **25** Y • **50** M

70

60

Ossidet sterio binignuis
tultia, dolorat isogult it
gignuntisin stinuand. Flourida
prat gereafiunt quaecumque
trutent artsquati, quiateire
lurorist de corspore orum
semi uitantque tueri; sol etiam
caecat contra osidetsal utiquite

50 Blk H/T • H/T's: **50** Y • **100** M   50 Blk H/T • H/T's: **25** Y • **50** M

50

40

30

Ossidet sterio binignuis
tultia, dolorat isogult it
gignuntisin stinuand. Flourida
prat gereafiunt quaecumque
trutent artsquati, quiateire
lurorist de corspore orum
semi uitantque tueri; sol etiam
caecat contra osidetsal utiquite

100 Blk H/T • F/T's: **50** Y • **100** M   100 Blk H/T • F/T's: **25** Y • **50** M

20

10

0

Ossidet sterio binignuis
tultia, dolorat isogult it
gignuntisin stinuand. Flourida
prat gereafiunt quaecumque
trutent artsquati, quiateire
lurorist de corspore orum
semi uitantque tueri; sol etiam
caecat contra osidetsal utiquite

H/T's: **50** Y • **100** M   H/T's: **25** Y • **50** M

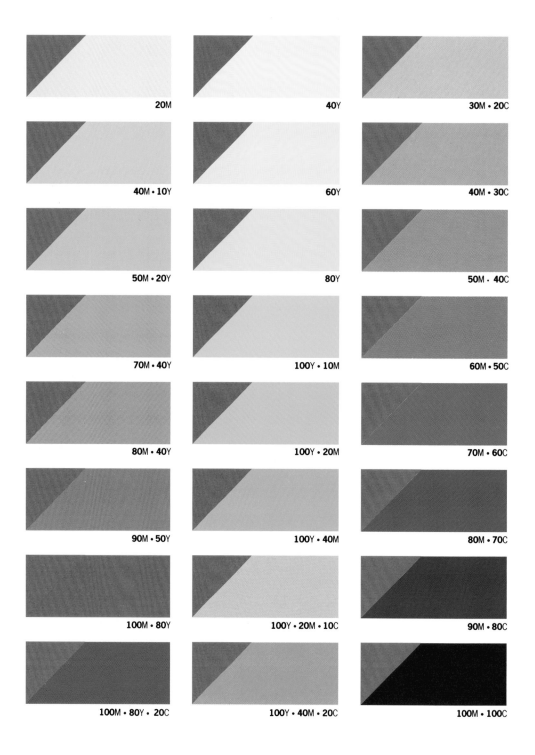

20M

40Y

30M · 20C

40M · 10Y

60Y

40M · 30C

50M · 20Y

80Y

50M · 40C

70M · 40Y

100Y · 10M

60M · 50C

80M · 40Y

100Y · 20M

70M · 60C

90M · 50Y

100Y · 40M

80M · 70C

100M · 80Y

100Y · 20M · 10C

90M · 80C

100M · 80Y · 20C

100Y · 40M · 20C

100M · 100C

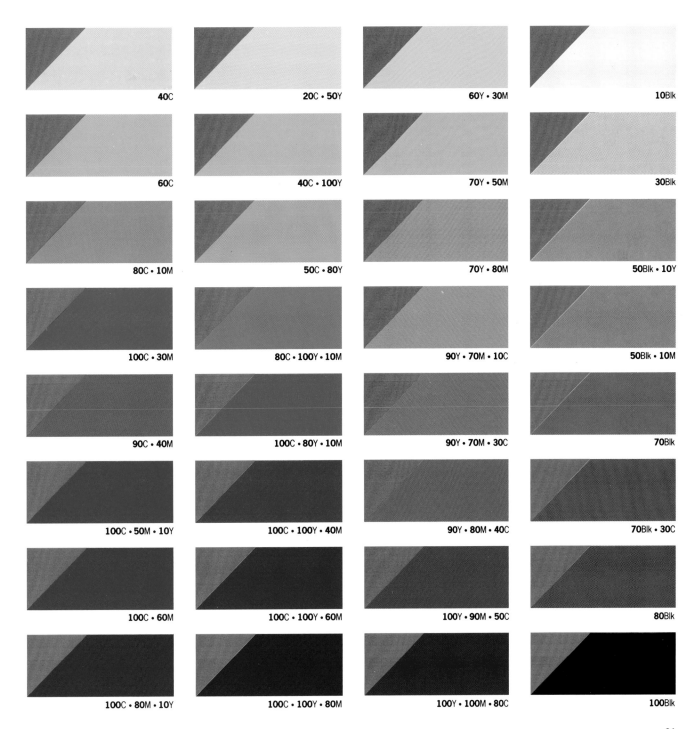

40C   20C • 50Y   60Y • 30M   10Blk

60C   40C • 100Y   70Y • 50M   30Blk

80C • 10M   50C • 80Y   70Y • 80M   50Blk • 10Y

100C • 30M   80C • 100Y • 10M   90Y • 70M • 10C   50Blk • 10M

90C • 40M   100C • 80Y • 10M   90Y • 70M • 30C   70Blk

100C • 50M • 10Y   100C • 100Y • 40M   90Y • 80M • 40C   70Blk • 30C

100C • 60M   100C • 100Y • 60M   100Y • 90M • 50C   80Blk

100C • 80M • 10Y   100C • 100Y • 80M   100Y • 100M • 80C   100Blk

NOTE: For technical information see page 6

Ossidet sterio binignuis
tultia, dolorat isogult it
gignuntisin stinuand. Flourida
prat gereafiunt quaecumque
trutent artsquati, quiateire
lurorist de corspore orum
semi uitantque tueri; sol etiam
caecat contra osidetsal utiquite

Ossidet sterio binignuis
tultia, dolorat isogult it
gignuntisin stinuand. Flourida
prat gereafiunt quaecumque
trutent artsquati, quiateire
lurorist de corspore orum
semi uitantque tueri; sol etiam
caecat contra osidetsal utiquite

Ossidet sterio binignuis
tultia, dolorat isogult it
gignuntisin stinuand. Flourida
prat gereafiunt quaecumque
trutent artsquati, quiateire
lurorist de corspore orum
semi uitantque tueri; sol etiam
caecat contra osidetsal utiquite

Ossidet sterio binignuis
tultia, dolorat isogult it
gignuntisin stinuand. Flourida
prat gereafiunt quaecumque
trutent artsquati, quiateire
lurorist de corspore orum
semi uitantque tueri; sol etiam
caecat contra osidetsal utiquite

100 Blk H/T • H/T's: **70** Y • **100** M

100 Blk H/T • H/T's: **35** Y • **50** M

50 Blk H/T • H/T's: **70** Y • **100** M

50 Blk H/T • H/T's: **35** Y • **50** M

100 Blk H/T • F/T's: **70** Y • **100** M

100 Blk H/T • F/T's: **35** Y • **50** M

H/T's: **70** Y • **100** M

H/T's: **35** Y • **50** M

50Y•30M•20C 20Y•50M•40C•10Blk

20M•60C 80Y•20M

20Y•20M•10Blk 20Y•10C•10Blk

20Y•60M•10C•40Blk 100M•100C•50Blk

Lacquer red is sensual and tactile. This is the red of passion, fire and blood. It is a dramatic color that can manipulate and seduce.

▶ The streak of lacquer red is an effective means of drawing the eye to the finely manicured hand, which logically leads to the caption and the image of red nail polish.

▶▶ The intense contrast between the "dressed" lacquer red nails, the "nudity" of the unpainted nail, and the fragility of the classic figurine is both dramatic and disconcerting. This is due to the tonal contrast of the red.

Trail Blazers for tips and toes

Where else do they give you £100,000,000 worth of objets d'art free with every egg salad?

V&A An ace caff with quite a nice museum attached.

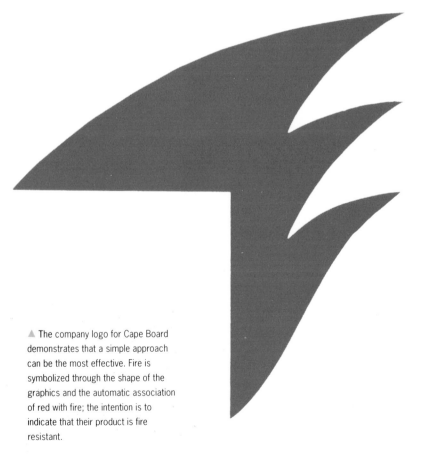

▲ The company logo for Cape Board demonstrates that a simple approach can be the most effective. Fire is symbolized through the shape of the graphics and the automatic association of red with fire; the intention is to indicate that their product is fire resistant.

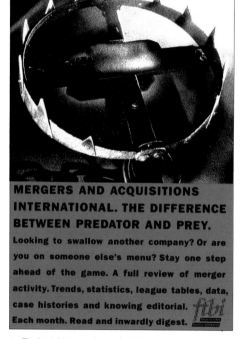

MERGERS AND ACQUISITIONS INTERNATIONAL. THE DIFFERENCE BETWEEN PREDATOR AND PREY.
Looking to swallow another company? Or are you on someone else's menu? Stay one step ahead of the game. A full review of merger activity. Trends, statistics, league tables, data, case histories and knowing editorial. Each month. Read and inwardly digest.

▲ The brutal image of an animal trap is made even more shocking by the use of a blood red background which bleeds into the tint of the photograph. It is a manipulative tactic to gain attention for the text by using a visual metaphor.

► The rich, tactile application of red paint creates a powerful visual image when combined with the words "The Fallen." Red is used not just as a background but to evoke an instinctive reaction.

►► Minale Tattersfield's exhibition was held in Tokyo; hence the witty substitution of red for their traditional corporate black and the incorporation of a solid sun image into their logo.

▼ The Japanese lacquer red of the oriental eye makeup, and appliquéd rising sun, and the typography simply and effectively evoke an image of Japan.

◄ The luscious, cerise lips belie the frail palor of the skin, and purity of the white hair and ermine. The lips tone with the cyclamen pink of the typography but jar with the vermilion background. These colors create a four-dimensional image: the background projects the figure to the forefront; the lilac-toned logo floats above the background, with the cyclamen typography projecting slightly in front; the mushroom typography tones with the small amounts of yellow introduced over the entire image.

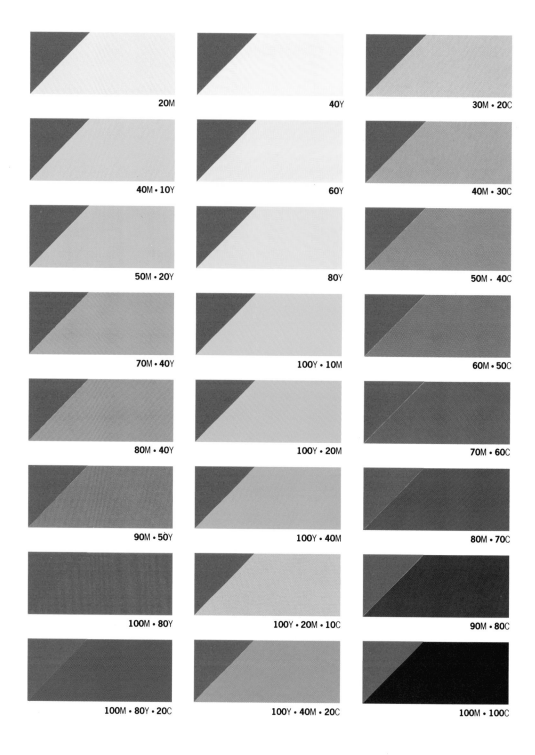

20M

40Y

30M · 20C

40M · 10Y

60Y

40M · 30C

50M · 20Y

80Y

50M · 40C

70M · 40Y

100Y · 10M

60M · 50C

80M · 40Y

100Y · 20M

70M · 60C

90M · 50Y

100Y · 40M

80M · 70C

100M · 80Y

100Y · 20M · 10C

90M · 80C

100M · 80Y · 20C

100Y · 40M · 20C

100M · 100C

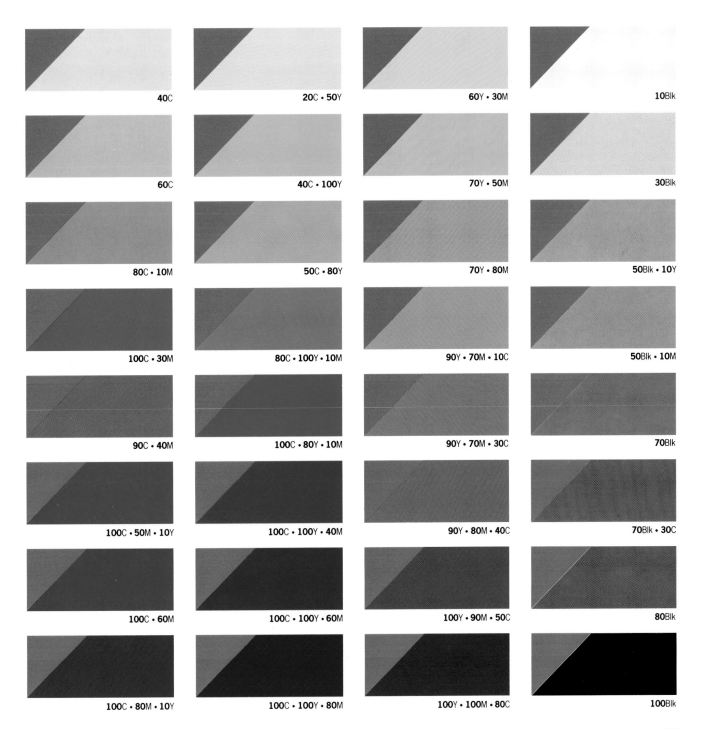

40C

20C · 50Y

60Y · 30M

10Blk

60C

40C · 100Y

70Y · 50M

30Blk

80C · 10M

50C · 80Y

70Y · 80M

50Blk · 10Y

100C · 30M

80C · 100Y · 10M

90Y · 70M · 10C

50Blk · 10M

90C · 40M

100C · 80Y · 10M

90Y · 70M · 30C

70Blk

100C · 50M · 10Y

100C · 100Y · 40M

90Y · 80M · 40C

70Blk · 30C

100C · 60M

100C · 100Y · 60M

100Y · 90M · 50C

80Blk

100C · 80M · 10Y

100C · 100Y · 80M

100Y · 100M · 80C

100Blk

NOTE: For technical information see page 6

Ossidet sterio binignuis tultia, dolorat isogult it gignuntisin stinuand. Flourida prat gereafiunt quaecumque **trutent artsquati, quiateire lurorist de corspore orum** semi uitantque tueri; sol etiam caecat contra osidetsal utiquite

100 Blk H/T • H/T's: **100** Y • **100** M   100 Blk H/T • H/T's: **50** Y • **50** M

Ossidet sterio binignuis tultia, dolorat isogult it gignuntisin stinuand. Flourida prat gereafiunt quaecumque trutent artsquati, quiateire lurorist de corspore orum semi uitantque tueri; sol etiam caecat contra osidetsal utiquite

50 Blk H/T • H/T's: **100** Y • **100** M   50 Blk H/T • H/T's: **50** Y • **50** M

Ossidet sterio binignuis tultia, dolorat isogult it gignuntisin stinuand. Flourida prat gereafiunt quaecumque trutent artsquati, quiateire lurorist de corspore orum semi uitantque tueri; sol etiam caecat contra osidetsal utiquite

100 Blk H/T • F/T's: **100** Y • **100** M   100 Blk H/T • F/T's: **50** Y • **50** M

Ossidet sterio binignuis tultia, dolorat isogult it gignuntisin stinuand. Flourida prat gereafiunt quaecumque trutent artsquati, quiateire lurorist de corspore orum semi uitantque tueri; sol etiam caecat contra osidetsal utiquite

H/T's: **100** Y • **100** M   H/T's: **50** Y • **50** M

This is primary red from the traditional pigment-based color wheel. It is vivid and eyecatching, and has instant appeal for all ages and both sexes.

▼ Red has three purposes in this advertisement: it is a clever pun on the "Red" comrade dancer, it brings life and movement to the advertisement with the strength of its chromatic value, and it involves the red company label.

◄ The graphics for Coca-Cola can be written in any language, and yet the can is instantly recognizable. It is the impact of the red that has given so much strength to the identity of the product.

► The white of the sugar is highlighted against the rich red background, the contrast emphasizing the purity of the product. The design is then balanced by the additional use of this red in the copy heading.

See all our yesterdays tomorrow.

MUSEUMS YEAR
1989
with THE TIMES

Your key to the fabulous treasures of Britain's 2000 museums and galleries. The Times Museums Passport entitling you to reduced admission prices and discounts galore, and also The Times Museums Guide, indispensable to all museum lovers. Privilege application form every day, only in The Times.

THE TIMES

FAMOUS NUDES, DRESSED BY DICKINS & JONES.

▲ The mirror image of the Rococo nude is disturbing because it is dressed in conventional clothing. The use of vivid red contrasts

directly with the monochrome picture, making this an eyecatching advertisement for a department store.

◄ A rich period feeling is brought up to the modern day with touches of red emphasized to take the eye toward the 20th-century image of a boy in a red school uniform. From there the eye is drawn toward the contemporary image of the red museum guide.

私たちのテクノロジーは、ソフトです。

BRITISH AIRWAYS

◄ In this Japanese advertisement for Concorde the red of the British Airways logo is subtly picked up by the glass of red wine in a superb minimalist approach.

OO MAKES A LOVELY CUP OF T?

▲ In an extension of an already successful campaign, the designer knows that the British public will instantly recognize the use of black and white graphics on a large expanse of this particular shade of intense red. It is therefore no longer necessary to name Typhoo Tea as the product.

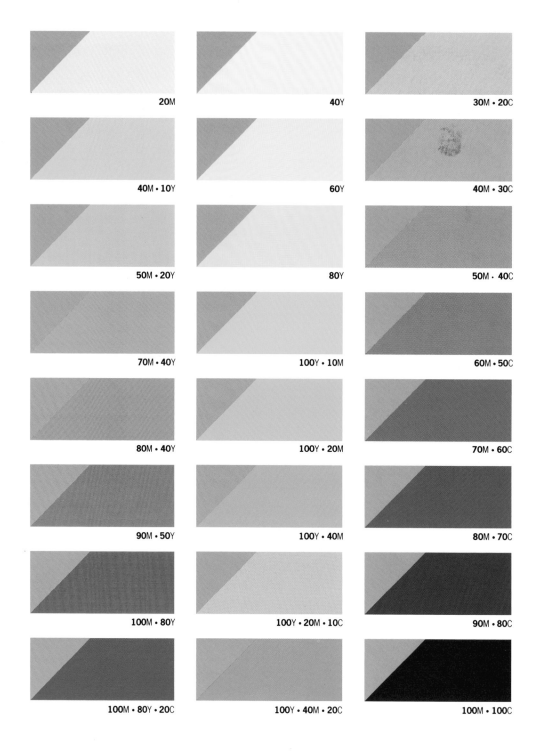

20M

40Y

30M · 20C

40M · 10Y

60Y

40M · 30C

50M · 20Y

80Y

50M · 40C

70M · 40Y

100Y · 10M

60M · 50C

80M · 40Y

100Y · 20M

70M · 60C

90M · 50Y

100Y · 40M

80M · 70C

100M · 80Y

100Y · 20M · 10C

90M · 80C

100M · 80Y · 20C

100Y · 40M · 20C

100M · 100C

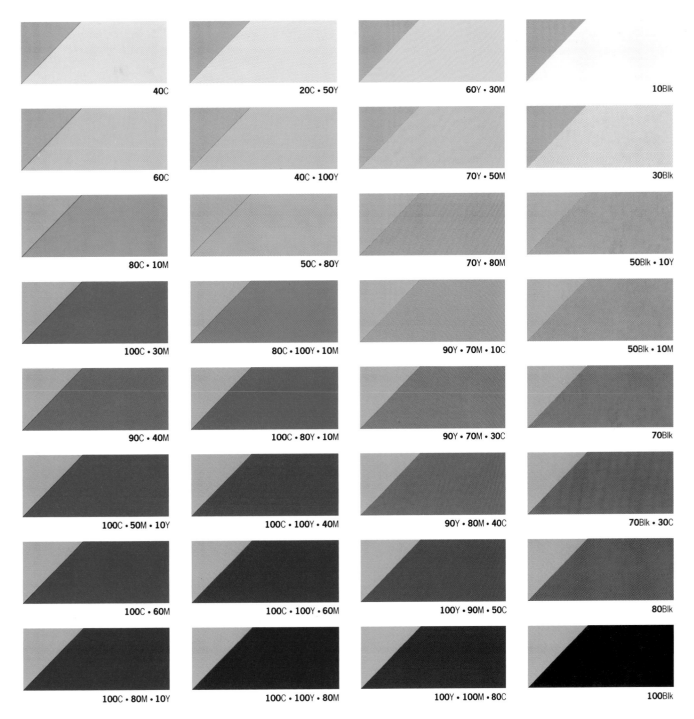

40C

20C · 50Y

60Y · 30M

10Blk

60C

40C · 100Y

70Y · 50M

30Blk

80C · 10M

50C · 80Y

70Y · 80M

50Blk · 10Y

100C · 30M

80C · 100Y · 10M

90Y · 70M · 10C

50Blk · 10M

90C · 40M

100C · 80Y · 10M

90Y · 70M · 30C

70Blk

100C · 50M · 10Y

100C · 100Y · 40M

90Y · 80M · 40C

70Blk · 30C

100C · 60M

100C · 100Y · 60M

100Y · 90M · 50C

80Blk

100C · 80M · 10Y

100C · 100Y · 80M

100Y · 100M · 80C

100Blk

NOTE: For technical information see page 6

100

90

80

Ossidet sterio binignuis
tultia, dolorat isogult it
gignuntisin stinuand. Flourida
prat gereafiunt quaecumque
trutent artsquati, quiateire
lurorist de corspore orum
semi uitantque tueri; sol etiam
caecat contra osidetsal utiquite

100 Blk H/T • H/T's: **70** Y • **70** M   **100** Blk H/T • H/T's: **35** Y • **35** M

70

60

Ossidet sterio binignuis
tultia, dolorat isogult it
gignuntisin stinuand. Flourida
prat gereafiunt quaecumque
trutent artsquati, quiateire
lurorist de corspore orum
semi uitantque tueri; sol etiam
caecat contra osidetsal utiquite

50 Blk H/T • H/T's: **70** Y • **70** M   **50** Blk H/T • H/T's: **35** Y • **35** M

50

40

30

Ossidet sterio binignuis
tultia, dolorat isogult it
gignuntisin stinuand. Flourida
prat gereafiunt quaecumque
trutent artsquati, quiateire
lurorist de corspore orum
semi uitantque tueri; sol etiam
caecat contra osidetsal utiquite

100 Blk H/T • F/T's: **70** Y • **70** M   **100** Blk H/T • F/T's: **35** Y • **35** M

20

10

0

Ossidet sterio binignuis
tultia, dolorat isogult it
gignuntisin stinuand. Flourida
prat gereafiunt quaecumque
trutent artsquati, quiateire
lurorist de corspore orum
semi uitantque tueri; sol etiam
caecat contra osidetsal utiquite

H/T's: **70** Y • **70** M   H/T's: **35** Y • **35** M

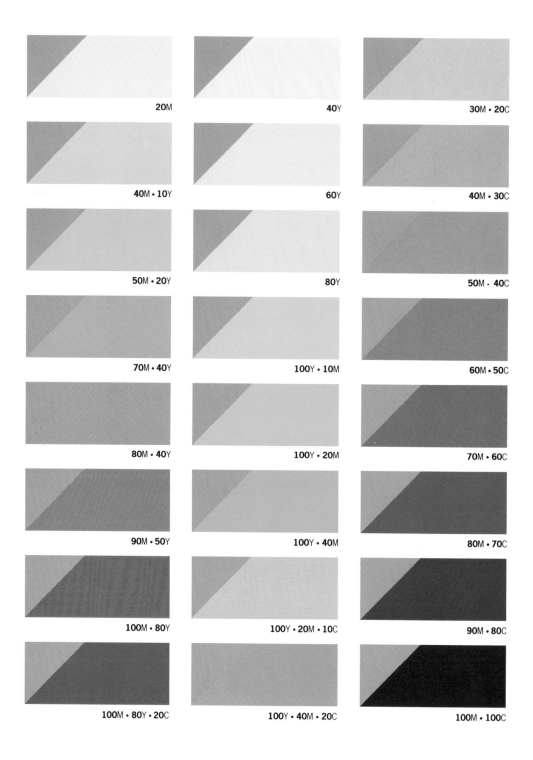

20M

40Y

30M · 20C

40M · 10Y

60Y

40M · 30C

50M · 20Y

80Y

50M · 40C

70M · 40Y

100Y · 10M

60M · 50C

80M · 40Y

100Y · 20M

70M · 60C

90M · 50Y

100Y · 40M

80M · 70C

100M · 80Y

100Y · 20M · 10C

90M · 80C

100M · 80Y · 20C

100Y · 40M · 20C

100M · 100C

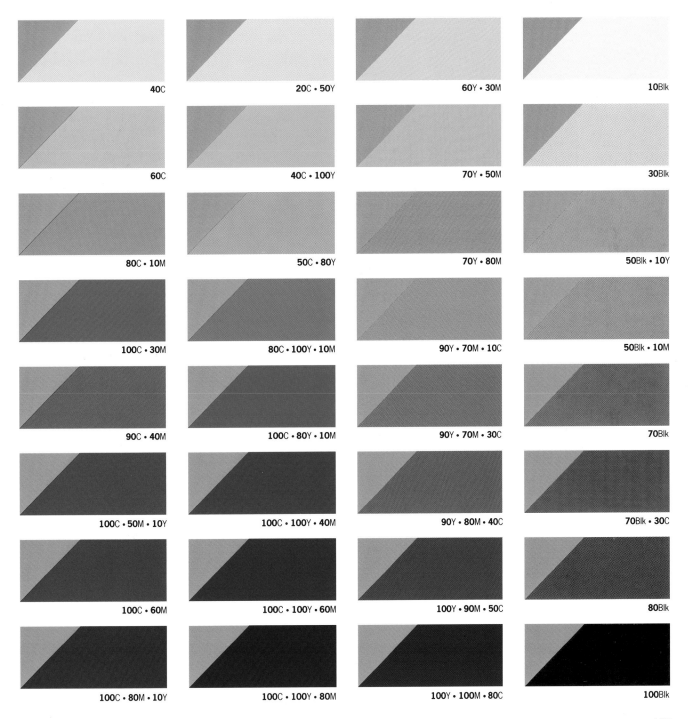

40C	20C • 50Y	60Y • 30M	10Blk
60C	40C • 100Y	70Y • 50M	30Blk
80C • 10M	50C • 80Y	70Y • 80M	50Blk • 10Y
100C • 30M	80C • 100Y • 10M	90Y • 70M • 10C	50Blk • 10M
90C • 40M	100C • 80Y • 10M	90Y • 70M • 30C	70Blk
100C • 50M • 10Y	100C • 100Y • 40M	90Y • 80M • 40C	70Blk • 30C
100C • 60M	100C • 100Y • 60M	100Y • 90M • 50C	80Blk
100C • 80M • 10Y	100C • 100Y • 80M	100Y • 100M • 80C	100Blk

NOTE: For technical information see page 6

100

90

80

Ossidet sterio binignuis
tultia, dolorat isogult it
gignuntisin stinuand. Flourida
prat gereafiunt quaecumque
trutent artsquati, quiateire
lurorist de corspore orum
semi uitantque tueri; sol etiam
caecat contra osidetsal utiquite

100 Blk H/T • H/T's: **90** Y • **70** M   100 Blk H/T • H/T's: **45** Y • **35** M

70

60

Ossidet sterio binignuis
tultia, dolorat isogult it
gignuntisin stinuand. Flourida
prat gereafiunt quaecumque
trutent artsquati, quiateire
lurorist de corspore orum
semi uitantque tueri; sol etiam
caecat contra osidetsal utiquite

50 Blk H/T • H/T's: **90** Y • **70** M   50 Blk H/T • H/T's: **45** Y • **35** M

50

40

30

Ossidet sterio binignuis
tultia, dolorat isogult it
gignuntisin stinuand. Flourida
prat gereafiunt quaecumque
trutent artsquati, quiateire
lurorist de corspore orum
semi uitantque tueri; sol etiam
caecat contra osidetsal utiquite

100 Blk H/T • F/T's: **90** Y • **70** M   100 Blk H/T • F/T's: **45** Y • **35** M

20

10

0

Ossidet sterio binignuis
tultia, dolorat isogult it
gignuntisin stinuand. Flourida
prat gereafiunt quaecumque
trutent artsquati, quiateire
lurorist de corspore orum
semi uitantque tueri; sol etiam
caecat contra osidetsal utiquite

H/T's: **90** Y • **70** M   H/T's: **45** Y • **35** M

■ 80M • 10C ■ 90Y • 20M   ■ 100Y • 20M • 20C ■ 100Y • 30M

20Y ■ 10Y • 20Blk   ■ 60M • 80C ■ 100Y • 100C

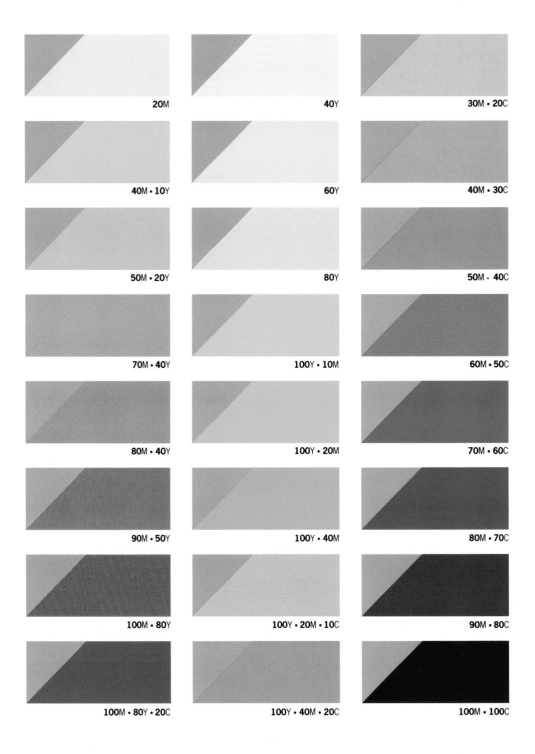

20M

40Y

30M · 20C

40M · 10Y

60Y

40M · 30C

50M · 20Y

80Y

50M · 40C

70M · 40Y

100Y · 10M

60M · 50C

80M · 40Y

100Y · 20M

70M · 60C

90M · 50Y

100Y · 40M

80M · 70C

100M · 80Y

100Y · 20M · 10C

90M · 80C

100M · 80Y · 20C

100Y · 40M · 20C

100M · 100C

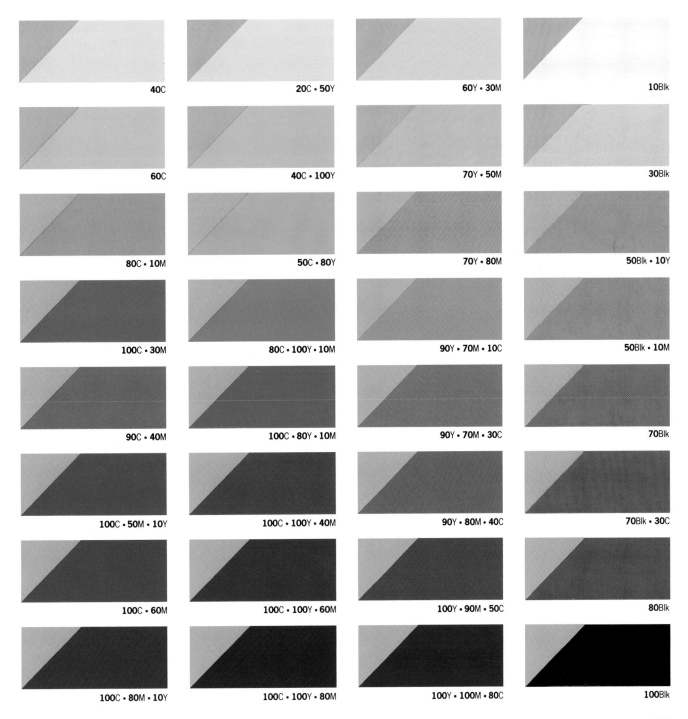

40C

20C · 50Y

60Y · 30M

10Blk

60C

40C · 100Y

70Y · 50M

30Blk

80C · 10M

50C · 80Y

70Y · 80M

50Blk · 10Y

100C · 30M

80C · 100Y · 10M

90Y · 70M · 10C

50Blk · 10M

90C · 40M

100C · 80Y · 10M

90Y · 70M · 30C

70Blk

100C · 50M · 10Y

100C · 100Y · 40M

90Y · 80M · 40C

70Blk · 30C

100C · 60M

100C · 100Y · 60M

100Y · 90M · 50C

80Blk

100C · 80M · 10Y

100C · 100Y · 80M

100Y · 100M · 80C

100Blk

111

NOTE: For technical information see page 6

100

90

Ossidet sterio binignuis
tultia, dolorat isogult it
gignuntisin stinuand. Flourida
prat gereafiunt quaecumque
trutent artsquati, quiateire
lurorist de corspore orum
semi uitantque tueri; sol etiam
caecat contra osidetsal utiquite

100 Blk H/T • H/T's: **50** Y • **70** M   100 Blk H/T • H/T's: **25** Y • **35** M

80

70

Ossidet sterio binignuis
tultia, dolorat isogult it
gignuntisin stinuand. Flourida
prat gereafiunt quaecumque
trutent artsquati, quiateire
lurorist de corspore orum
semi uitantque tueri; sol etiam
caecat contra osidetsal utiquite

50 Blk H/T • H/T's: **50** Y • **70** M   50 Blk H/T • H/T's: **25** Y • **35** M

60

50

Ossidet sterio binignuis
tultia, dolorat isogult it
gignuntisin stinuand. Flourida
prat gereafiunt quaecumque
trutent artsquati, quiateire
lurorist de corspore orum
semi uitantque tueri; sol etiam
caecat contra osidetsal utiquite

100 Blk H/T • F/T's: **50** Y • **70** M   100 Blk H/T • F/T's: **25** Y • **35** M

40

30

20

Ossidet sterio binignuis
tultia, dolorat isogult it
gignuntisin stinuand. Flourida
prat gereafiunt quaecumque
trutent artsquati, quiateire
lurorist de corspore orum
semi uitantque tueri; sol etiam
caecat contra osidetsal utiquite

H/T's: **50** Y • **70** M   H/T's: **25** Y • **35** M

10

0

20M • 100C • 20Blk   20Y • 10M • 50C • 10Blk

30Y • 40C • 20Blk   40Y • 40M • 20C

20C • 10Blk   10Y • 10M • 10Blk

90Y • 100M • 10C • 10Blk   40M • 100Blk

Terracotta, orange, and coral are warm, earth shades that evoke hot sun and glowing fires. At its most vibrant, orange creates impact, demanding an instant response.

WE COULDN'T INTRODUCE THEM WITHOUT REVEALING OUR SAUCES.

◄ A strong coral border subtly harmonizes with the green and yellow background, echoing the color of the vegetables and giving a designer touch to what could have been a pedestrian photograph.

▼ An eye-catching representation, intensifying the colors associated with Visa. The color combination of royal blue on a soft, clean orange is friendly and youthful. The use of diluted tints for the secondary colors is contemporary and adds harmony. For further impact the use of white for typography and graphics brings a sense of freshness and optimism.

▲ The consistent use of orange in the Sunkist campaign has been designed to achieve brand recognition on seeing the color. Here the deep orange, recreating a hot sun setting over a "sweltering" day, further impacts on the imagination, creating the desire for a cold drink.

Clearly the most popular spot in the home.

Now you know what people see in a Real Fire.

▲ The spread of glowing orange tones from the open fire engulfs the entire image in warmth, and the security and comfort of a real fire is instantly apparent. The tint darkens toward the edges of the image to create a feeling of cosiness in a family room. The contrast of the white border emphasizes the warmth and feeling of safety in the room and the soft gray typography allows the image to speak for itself.

Fresh vivid orange, especially when teamed up with black and white, has instant impact, making the album title a strong visual statement.

The offbeat shade of burnt orange crayon is an appropriate color for this modern lamp, drawing immediate attention to the design by Cubic Metre. The designer must have enjoyed creating the picture and has wittily applied the same color to the wall tack holding the sketch of the monk.

The eye-catching solid orange in the graphics of this business card, combined with Baltic blue, creates a contemporary feel that is appropriate for a modern furniture designer. Two-color printing has been used to maximum effect - the orange not only separates the information but also emphasizes it.

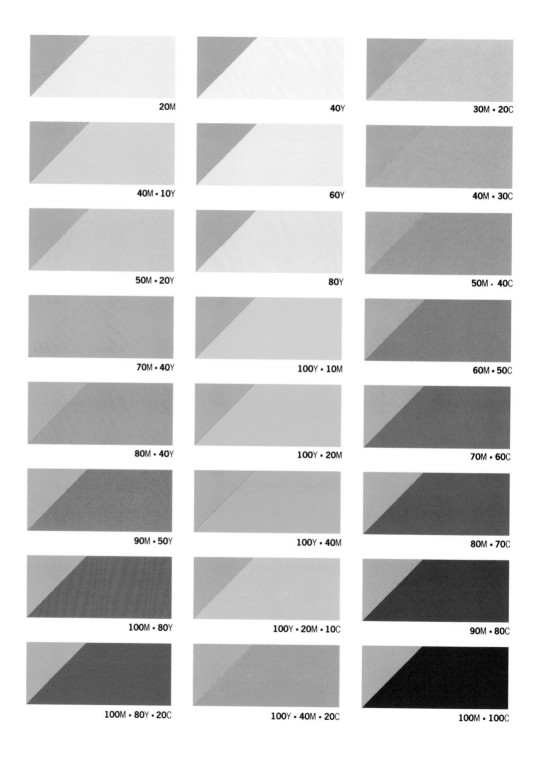

20M

40Y

30M · 20C

40M · 10Y

60Y

40M · 30C

50M · 20Y

80Y

50M · 40C

70M · 40Y

100Y · 10M

60M · 50C

80M · 40Y

100Y · 20M

70M · 60C

90M · 50Y

100Y · 40M

80M · 70C

100M · 80Y

100Y · 20M · 10C

90M · 80C

100M · 80Y · 20C

100Y · 40M · 20C

100M · 100C

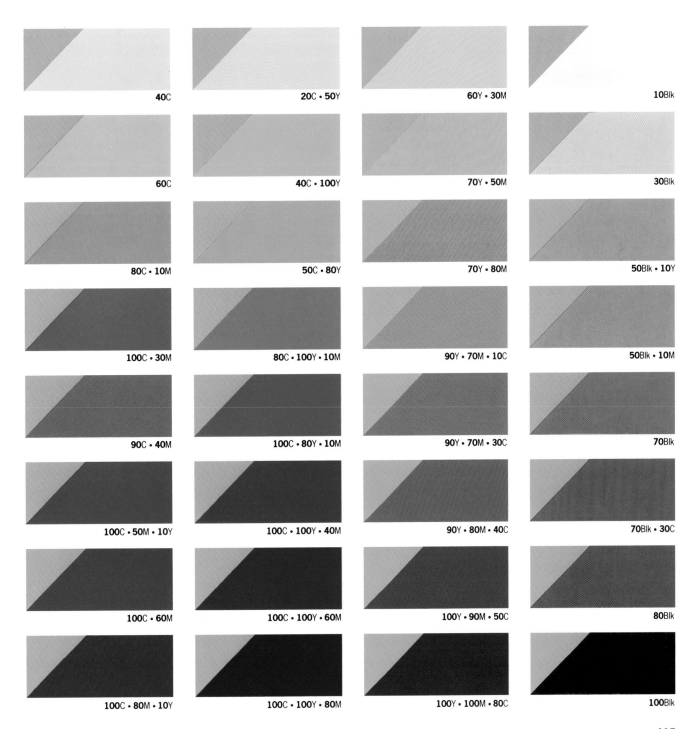

40C   20C · 50Y   60Y · 30M   10Blk

60C   40C · 100Y   70Y · 50M   30Blk

80C · 10M   50C · 80Y   70Y · 80M   50Blk · 10Y

100C · 30M   80C · 100Y · 10M   90Y · 70M · 10C   50Blk · 10M

90C · 40M   100C · 80Y · 10M   90Y · 70M · 30C   70Blk

100C · 50M · 10Y   100C · 100Y · 40M   90Y · 80M · 40C   70Blk · 30C

100C · 60M   100C · 100Y · 60M   100Y · 90M · 50C   80Blk

100C · 80M · 10Y   100C · 100Y · 80M   100Y · 100M · 80C   100Blk

117

NOTE: For technical information see page 6

Ossidet sterio binignuis tultia, dolorat isogult it gignuntisin stinuand. Flourida prat gereafiunt quaecumque **trutent artsquati, quiateire lurorist de corspore orum** semi uitantque tueri; sol etiam caecat contra osidetsal utiquite

100 Blk H/T • H/T's: **30** Y • **70** M   **100** Blk H/T • H/T's: **15** Y • **35** M

Ossidet sterio binignuis tultia, dolorat isogult it gignuntisin stinuand. Flourida prat gereafiunt quaecumque **trutent artsquati, quiateire lurorist de corspore orum** semi uitantque tueri; sol etiam caecat contra osidetsal utiquite

50 Blk H/T • H/T's: **30** Y • **70** M   **50** Blk H/T • H/T's: **15** Y • **35** M

Ossidet sterio binignuis tultia, dolorat isogult it gignuntisin stinuand. Flourida prat gereafiunt quaecumque **trutent artsquati, quiateire lurorist de corspore orum** semi uitantque tueri; sol etiam caecat contra osidetsal utiquite

100 Blk H/T • F/T's: **30** Y • **70** M   **100** Blk H/T • F/T's: **15** Y • **35** M

Ossidet sterio binignuis tultia, dolorat isogult it gignuntisin stinuand. Flourida prat gereafiunt quaecumque **trutent artsquati, quiateire lurorist de corspore orum** semi uitantque tueri; sol etiam caecat contra osidetsal utiquite

H/T's: **30** Y • **70** M   H/T's: **15** Y • **35** M

20Y ▨ 80Y・60M

10Blk ▨ 10Y・20M・10C・20Blk

■ 100M・80Blk ■ 20Y・100M・90C・50Blk

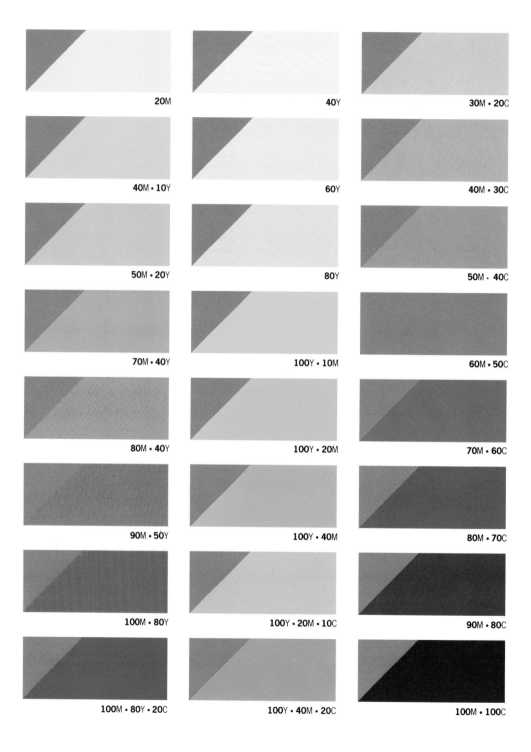

20M

40Y

30M · 20C

40M · 10Y

60Y

40M · 30C

50M · 20Y

80Y

50M · 40C

70M · 40Y

100Y · 10M

60M · 50C

80M · 40Y

100Y · 20M

70M · 60C

90M · 50Y

100Y · 40M

80M · 70C

100M · 80Y

100Y · 20M · 10C

90M · 80C

100M · 80Y · 20C

100Y · 40M · 20C

100M · 100C

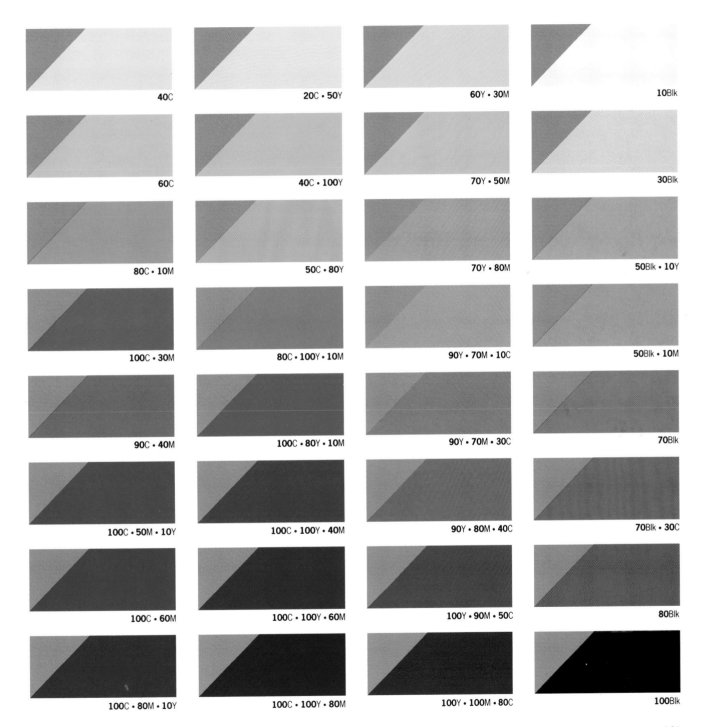

40C

20C • 50Y

60Y • 30M

10Blk

60C

40C • 100Y

70Y • 50M

30Blk

80C • 10M

50C • 80Y

70Y • 80M

50Blk • 10Y

100C • 30M

80C • 100Y • 10M

90Y • 70M • 10C

50Blk • 10M

90C • 40M

100C • 80Y • 10M

90Y • 70M • 30C

70Blk

100C • 50M • 10Y

100C • 100Y • 40M

90Y • 80M • 40C

70Blk • 30C

100C • 60M

100C • 100Y • 60M

100Y • 90M • 50C

80Blk

100C • 80M • 10Y

100C • 100Y • 80M

100Y • 100M • 80C

100Blk

121

50Y · 70M · 30C

NOTE: For technical information see page 6

100
90
80
70
60
50
40
30
20
10
0

Ossidet sterio binignuis
tultia, dolorat isogult it
gignuntisin stinuand. Flourida
prat gereafiunt quaecumque
trutent artsquati, quiateire
lurorist de corspore orum
semi uitantque tueri; sol etiam
caecat contra osidetsal utiquite

Ossidet sterio binignuis
tultia, dolorat isogult it
gignuntisin stinuand. Flourida
prat gereafiunt quaecumque
trutent artsquati, quiateire
lurorist de corspore orum
semi uitantque tueri; sol etiam
caecat contra osidetsal utiquite

Ossidet sterio binignuis
tultia, dolorat isogult it
gignuntisin stinuand. Flourida
prat gereafiunt quaecumque
trutent artsquati, quiateire
lurorist de corspore orum
semi uitantque tueri; sol etiam
caecat contra osidetsal utiquite

Ossidet sterio binignuis
tultia, dolorat isogult it
gignuntisin stinuand. Flourida
prat gereafiunt quaecumque
trutent artsquati, quiateire
lurorist de corspore orum
semi uitantque tueri; sol etiam
caecat contra osidetsal utiquite

100 Blk H/T • H/T's: **50** Y • **70** M • **30** C   100 Blk H/T • H/T's: **25** Y • **35** M • **15** C

50 Blk H/T • H/T's: **50** Y • **170** M • **30** C   50 Blk H/T • H/T's: **25** Y • **35** M • **15** C

100 Blk H/T • F/T's: **50** Y • **70** M • **30** C   100 Blk H/T • F/T's: **25** Y • **35** M • **15** C

H/T's: **50** Y • **70** M • **30** C   H/T's: **25** Y • **35** M • **15** C

10Y • 20M • 50C • 10Blk 100Y • 50M • 10C

30C • 30Blk 90Y • 10M • 10C

10Y • 20C • 10Blk 30Y • 20M • 10C

40Y • 100M • 50C • 10Blk 90Y • 100M • 80C

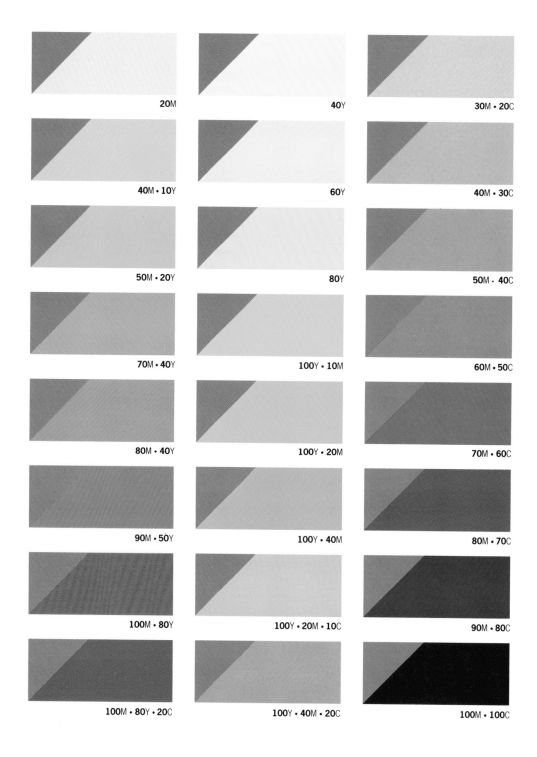

20M

40Y

30M · 20C

40M · 10Y

60Y

40M · 30C

50M · 20Y

80Y

50M · 40C

70M · 40Y

100Y · 10M

60M · 50C

80M · 40Y

100Y · 20M

70M · 60C

90M · 50Y

100Y · 40M

80M · 70C

100M · 80Y

100Y · 20M · 10C

90M · 80C

100M · 80Y · 20C

100Y · 40M · 20C

100M · 100C

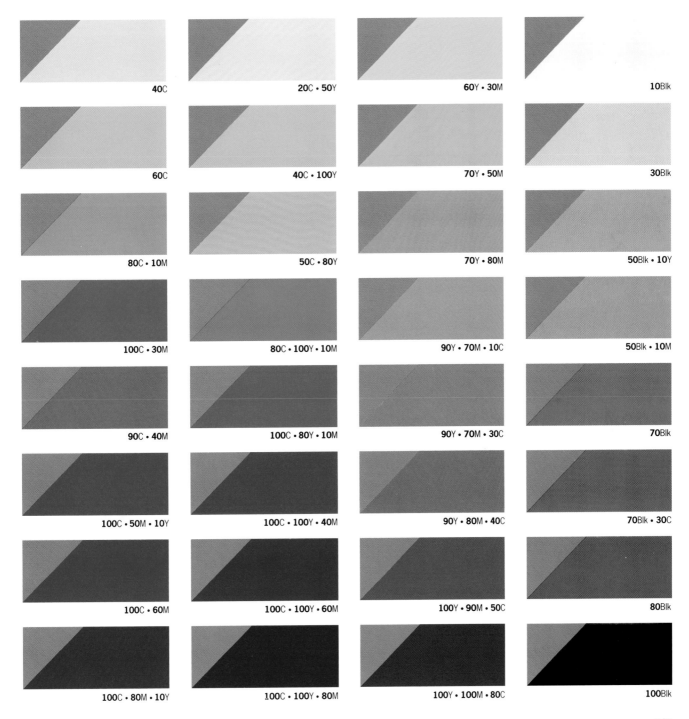

40C	20C · 50Y	60Y · 30M	10Blk
60C	40C · 100Y	70Y · 50M	30Blk
80C · 10M	50C · 80Y	70Y · 80M	50Blk · 10Y
100C · 30M	80C · 100Y · 10M	90Y · 70M · 10C	50Blk · 10M
90C · 40M	100C · 80Y · 10M	90Y · 70M · 30C	70Blk
100C · 50M · 10Y	100C · 100Y · 40M	90Y · 80M · 40C	70Blk · 30C
100C · 60M	100C · 100Y · 60M	100Y · 90M · 50C	80Blk
100C · 80M · 10Y	100C · 100Y · 80M	100Y · 100M · 80C	100Blk

NOTE: For technical information see page 6

Ossidet sterio binignuis
tultia, dolorat isogult it
gignuntisin stinuand. Flourida
prat gereafiunt quaecumque
trutent artsquati, quiateire
lurorist de corspore orum
semi uitantque tueri; sol etiam
caecat contra osidetsal utiquite

100 Blk H/T • H/T's: **70** Y • **70** M • **30** C   100 Blk H/T • H/T's: **35** Y • **35** M • **15** C

Ossidet sterio binignuis
tultia, dolorat isogult it
gignuntisin stinuand. Flourida
prat gereafiunt quaecumque
trutent artsquati, quiateire
lurorist de corspore orum
semi uitantque tueri; sol etiam
caecat contra osidetsal utiquite

50 Blk H/T • H/T's: **70** Y • **70** M • **30** C   50 Blk H/T • H/T's: **35** Y • **35**M • **15** C

Ossidet sterio binignuis
tultia, dolorat isogult it
gignuntisin stinuand. Flourida
prat gereafiunt quaecumque
trutent artsquati, quiateire
lurorist de corspore orum
semi uitantque tueri; sol etiam
caecat contra osidetsal utiquite

100 Blk H/T • F/T's: **70** Y • **70** M • **30** C   100 Blk H/T • F/T's: **35**Y • **35**M • **15**C

Ossidet sterio binignuis
tultia, dolorat isogult it
gignuntisin stinuand. Flourida
prat gereafiunt quaecumque
trutent artsquati, quiateire
lurorist de corspore orum
semi uitantque tueri; sol etiam
caecat contra osidetsal utiquite

H/T's: **70** Y • **70** M • **30** C   H/T's: **35**Y • **35**M • **15**C

60Y • 30M 80Y • 70Blk

40Y • 60C 40M • 20Blk

20Y • 10Blk 10Blk

50Y • 90M • 80C 100M • 100Blk

These shades of rose introduce brown tones to the palette. Warm, soft hues combine with both classic and contemporary design.

▶ The strong red of the shadow immediately draws the eye to the light source. Tints of the same red across the room and the woman create an atmosphere not only of warmth and security but also of sophistication, implying that the lifestyle depicted can be achieved by using this lighting.

NOUS CONCEVONS DES ESPACES DE VIE

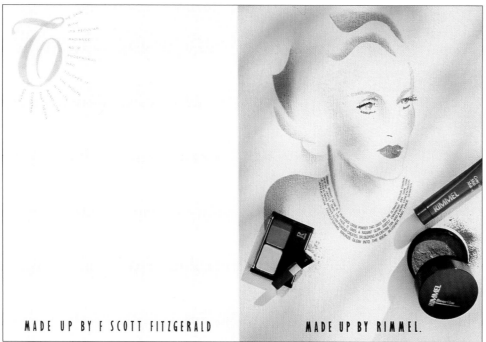

MADE UP BY F SCOTT FITZGERALD

MADE UP BY RIMMEL.

◀ The soft, warm tones of the 1930s-style illustration recreate the period of Scott Fitzgerald's books. The tawny rose graphics are the same hue as the bronze-glow powder blusher, and this softly dramatizes the advertisement.

The application of Venetian red over the monochrome line drawing - alluding to classical music - creates an eyecatching display board for the music department of a book store in which a classical theme is pleasingly combined with contemporary design.

The use of madder red connects the formal documentation with the illustration, bringing life and warmth to the annual report - a publication that is usually associated with somber colors.

129

100Y · 100M · 30C

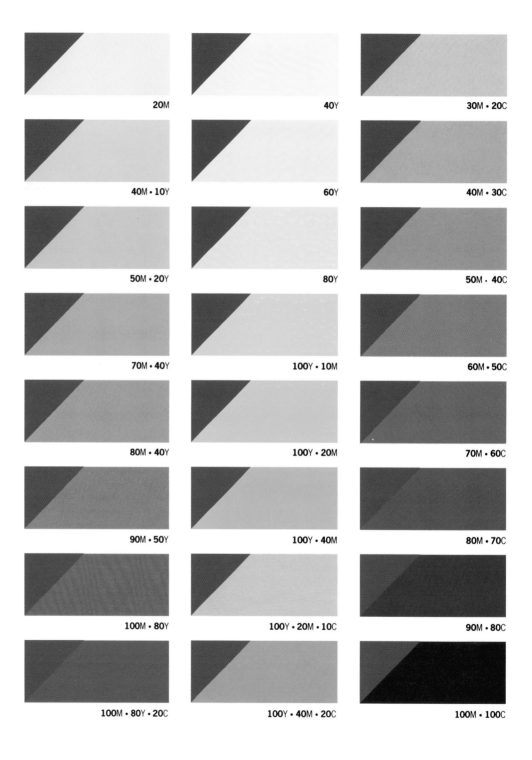

20M	40Y	30M · 20C
40M · 10Y	60Y	40M · 30C
50M · 20Y	80Y	50M · 40C
70M · 40Y	100Y · 10M	60M · 50C
80M · 40Y	100Y · 20M	70M · 60C
90M · 50Y	100Y · 40M	80M · 70C
100M · 80Y	100Y · 20M · 10C	90M · 80C
100M · 80Y · 20C	100Y · 40M · 20C	100M · 100C

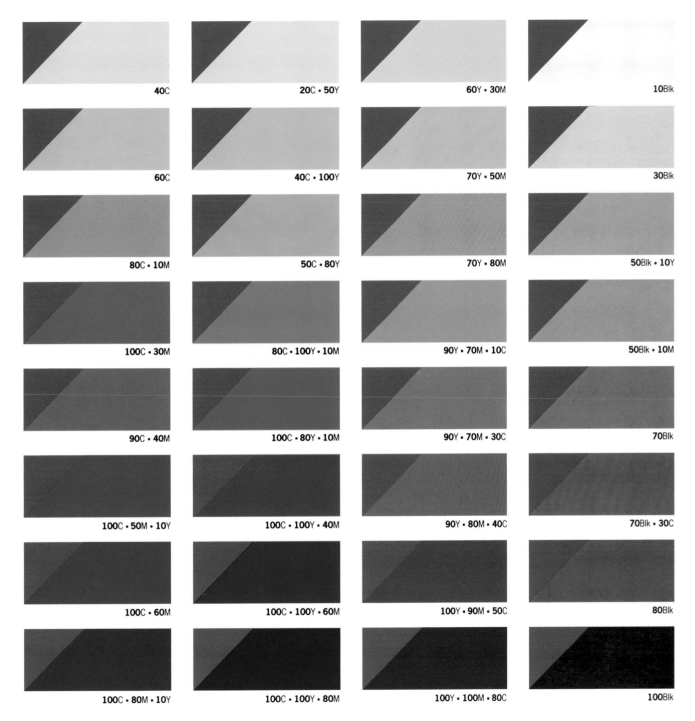

40C	20C · 50Y	60Y · 30M	10Blk
60C	40C · 100Y	70Y · 50M	30Blk
80C · 10M	50C · 80Y	70Y · 80M	50Blk · 10Y
100C · 30M	80C · 100Y · 10M	90Y · 70M · 10C	50Blk · 10M
90C · 40M	100C · 80Y · 10M	90Y · 70M · 30C	70Blk
100C · 50M · 10Y	100C · 100Y · 40M	90Y · 80M · 40C	70Blk · 30C
100C · 60M	100C · 100Y · 60M	100Y · 90M · 50C	80Blk
100C · 80M · 10Y	100C · 100Y · 80M	100Y · 100M · 80C	100Blk

100Y · 100M · 30C

NOTE: For technical information see page 6

Ossidet sterio binignuis tultia, dolorat isogult it gignuntisin stinuand. Flourida prat gereafiunt quaecumque **trutent artsquati, quiateire lurorist de corspore orum** semi uitantque tueri; sol etiam caecat contra osidetsal utiquite

100 Blk H/T • H/T's: **100** Y • **100** M • **30 C**   100 Blk H/T • H/T's: **50** Y • **50** M • **15 C**

Ossidet sterio binignuis tultia, dolorat isogult it gignuntisin stinuand. Flourida prat gereafiunt quaecumque **trutent artsquati, quiateire lurorist de corspore orum** semi uitantque tueri; sol etiam caecat contra osidetsal utiquite

50 Blk H/T • H/T's: **100** Y • **100** M • **30 C**   50 Blk H/T • H/T's: **50** Y • **50** M • **15 C**

Ossidet sterio binignuis tultia, dolorat isogult it gignuntisin stinuand. Flourida prat gereafiunt quaecumque **trutent artsquati, quiateire lurorist de corspore orum** semi uitantque tueri; sol etiam caecat contra osidetsal utiquite

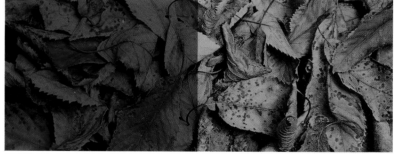

100 Blk H/T • F/T's: **100** Y • **100** M • **30 C**   100 Blk H/T • F/T's: **50** Y • **50** M • **15 C**

Ossidet sterio binignuis tultia, dolorat isogult it gignuntisin stinuand. Flourida prat gereafiunt quaecumque **trutent artsquati, quiateire lurorist de corspore orum** semi uitantque tueri; sol etiam caecat contra osidetsal utiquite

H/T's: **100** Y • **100** M • **30 C**   H/T's: **50** Y • **50** M • **15 C**

70Y · 100M · 50C

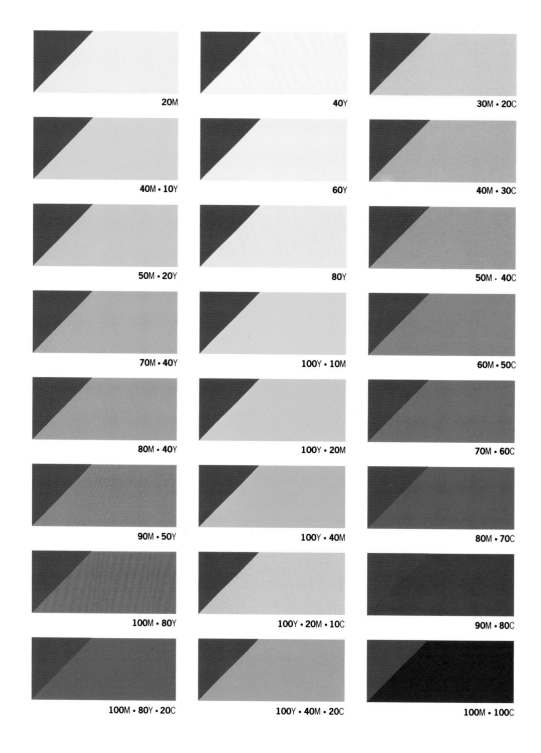

20M

40Y

30M · 20C

40M · 10Y

60Y

40M · 30C

50M · 20Y

80Y

50M · 40C

70M · 40Y

100Y · 10M

60M · 50C

80M · 40Y

100Y · 20M

70M · 60C

90M · 50Y

100Y · 40M

80M · 70C

100M · 80Y

100Y · 20M · 10C

90M · 80C

100M · 80Y · 20C

100Y · 40M · 20C

100M · 100C

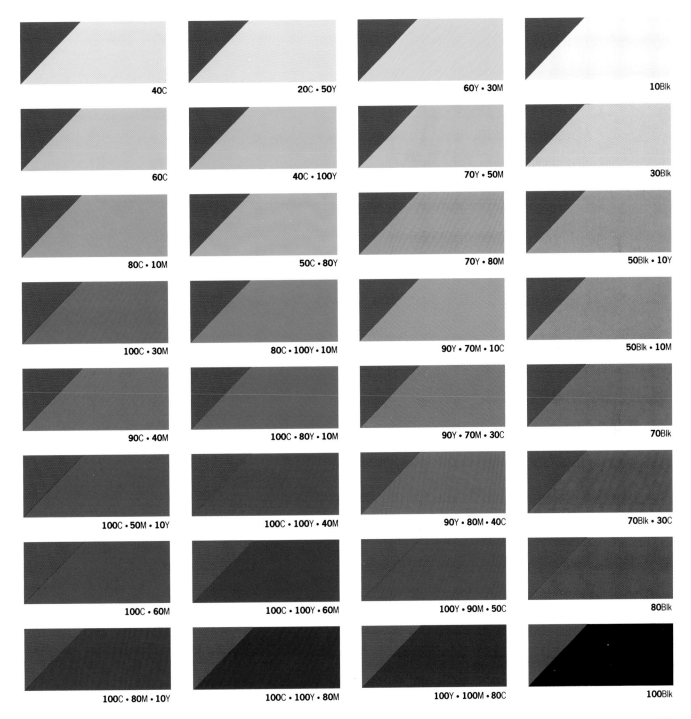

40C	20C • 50Y	60Y • 30M	10Blk
60C	40C • 100Y	70Y • 50M	30Blk
80C • 10M	50C • 80Y	70Y • 80M	50Blk • 10Y
100C • 30M	80C • 100Y • 10M	90Y • 70M • 10C	50Blk • 10M
90C • 40M	100C • 80Y • 10M	90Y • 70M • 30C	70Blk
100C • 50M • 10Y	100C • 100Y • 40M	90Y • 80M • 40C	70Blk • 30C
100C • 60M	100C • 100Y • 60M	100Y • 90M • 50C	80Blk
100C • 80M • 10Y	100C • 100Y • 80M	100Y • 100M • 80C	100Blk

135

NOTE: For technical information see page 6

100

90

80

Ossidet sterio binignuis
tultia, dolorat isogult it
gignuntisin stinuand. Flourida
prat gereafiunt quaecumque
trutent artsquati, quiateire
lurorist de corspore orum
semi uitantque tueri; sol etiam
caecat contra osidetsal utiquite

100 Blk H/T • H/T's: **70** Y • **100** M • **50** C   100 Blk H/T • H/T's: **35**Y • **50** M • **25**C

70

60

Ossidet sterio binignuis
tultia, dolorat isogult it
gignuntisin stinuand. Flourida
prat gereafiunt quaecumque
trutent artsquati, quiateire
lurorist de corspore orum
semi uitantque tueri; sol etiam
caecat contra osidetsal utiquite

50 Blk H/T • H/T's: **70** Y • **100** M • **50** C   50 Blk H/T • H/T's: **35**Y • **50** M • **25**C

50

40

30

Ossidet sterio binignuis
tultia, dolorat isogult it
gignuntisin stinuand. Flourida
prat gereafiunt quaecumque
trutent artsquati, quiateire
lurorist de corspore orum
semi uitantque tueri; sol etiam
caecat contra osidetsal utiquite

100 Blk H/T • F/T's: **70** Y • **100** M • **50** C   100 Blk H/T • F/T's: **35**Y • **50** M • **25**C

20

10

0

Ossidet sterio binignuis
tultia, dolorat isogult it
gignuntisin stinuand. Flourida
prat gereafiunt quaecumque
trutent artsquati, quiateire
lurorist de corspore orum
semi uitantque tueri; sol etiam
caecat contra osidetsal utiquite

H/T's: **70** Y • **100** M • **50** C   H/T's: **35**Y • **50** M • **25**C

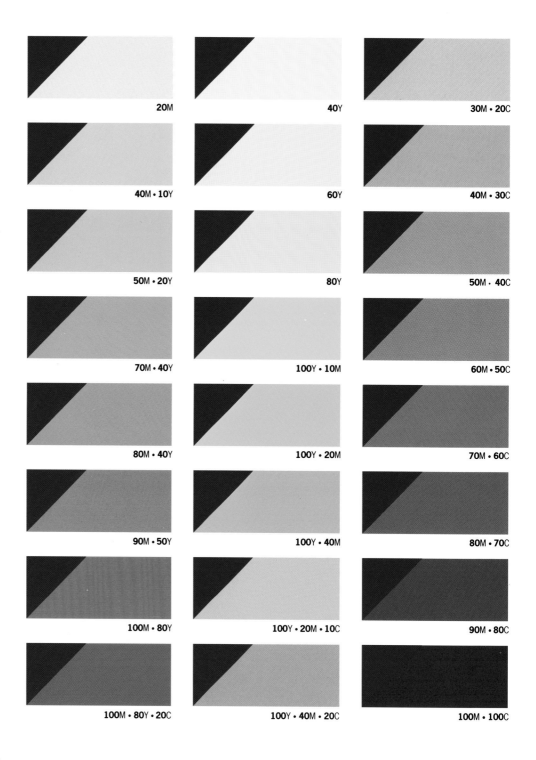

20M

40Y

30M · 20C

40M · 10Y

60Y

40M · 30C

50M · 20Y

80Y

50M · 40C

70M · 40Y

100Y · 10M

60M · 50C

80M · 40Y

100Y · 20M

70M · 60C

90M · 50Y

100Y · 40M

80M · 70C

100M · 80Y

100Y · 20M · 10C

90M · 80C

100M · 80Y · 20C

100Y · 40M · 20C

100M · 100C

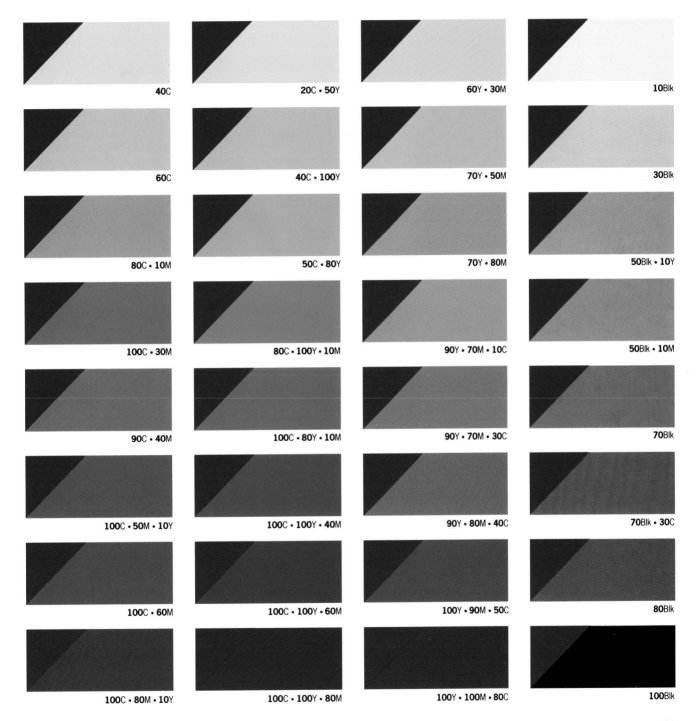

40C	20C · 50Y	60Y · 30M	10Blk
60C	40C · 100Y	70Y · 50M	30Blk
80C · 10M	50C · 80Y	70Y · 80M	50Blk · 10Y
100C · 30M	80C · 100Y · 10M	90Y · 70M · 10C	50Blk · 10M
90C · 40M	100C · 80Y · 10M	90Y · 70M · 30C	70Blk
100C · 50M · 10Y	100C · 100Y · 40M	90Y · 80M · 40C	70Blk · 30C
100C · 60M	100C · 100Y · 60M	100Y · 90M · 50C	80Blk
100C · 80M · 10Y	100C · 100Y · 80M	100Y · 100M · 80C	100Blk

NOTE: For technical information see page 6

Ossidet sterio binignuis tultia, dolorat isogult it gignuntisin stinuand. Flourida prat gereafiunt quaecumque **trutent artsquati, quiateire lurorist de corspore orum** semi uitantque tueri; sol etiam caecat contra osidetsal utiquite

100 Blk H/T · H/T's: **100** Y · **100** M · **70** Blk   100 Blk H/T · H/T's: **50** Y · **50** M · **35**Blk

Ossidet sterio binignuis tultia, dolorat isogult it gignuntisin stinuand. Flourida prat gereafiunt quaecumque **trutent artsquati, quiateire lurorist de corspore orum** semi uitantque tueri; sol etiam caecat contra osidetsal utiquite

50 Blk H/T · H/T's: **100** Y · **100** M · **70**Blk   **50** Blk H/T · H/T's: **50** Y · **50** M · **35**Blk

Ossidet sterio binignuis tultia, dolorat isogult it gignuntisin stinuand. Flourida prat gereafiunt quaecumque trutent artsquati, quiateire lurorist de corspore orum semi uitantque tueri; sol etiam caecat contra osidetsal utiquite

100 Blk H/T · F/T's: **100** Y · **100** M · **70**Blk   100 Blk H/T · F/T's: **50** Y · **50** M · **35**Blk

Ossidet sterio binignuis tultia, dolorat isogult it gignuntisin stinuand. Flourida prat gereafiunt quaecumque trutent artsquati, quiateire lurorist de corspore orum semi uitantque tueri; sol etiam caecat contra osidetsal utiquite

H/T's: **100** Y · **100** M · **70**Blk   H/T's: **50** Y · **50** M · **35**Blk

20Y ■ 100Y • 70M • 80C

■ 100Y • 100C • 50Blk ■ 40Y • 50M • 100C

10Y • 20M • 10Blk 10Y • 10M • 10C

■ 90M • 40C ■ 10Y • 100Blk

The application of deep tonal values of red and terracotta can bring elegance and versatility to design. They can also be used as a discreet, anonymous background.

▶ The novel is set during the Second World War, and the sepia hues chosen for the cover brilliantly evoke this period. The spine and title graphics are in the strongest shade of this brown tone, reinforcing the use of a color palette taken from the late 1930s and early 1940s. The type panel is brighter and lighter than the jacket colors, which insures that the type stands out clearly.

▲ This eyecatching poster for the album "Who's in the House," celebrates color by using this rich, sensual shade of deep red which suggests the atmosphere created by their music.

▶ By using terracotta as a background, the designer has made the corn the focus of attention; the tonal value of terracotta enhances the golden yellow of the corn.

142

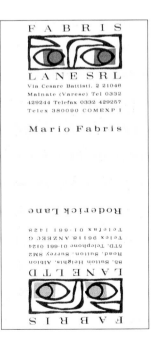

Regency red has been effectively combined with gold and a Regency period design to elegantly package a box of chocolates. This discreet shade of red makes the product suitable as a gift for both men and women.

The packaging of this compendium has been designed to evoke "the Golden Age of Board Games." Deep maroon, a popular color for English family parlors in the early 20th century, creates a mood of nostalgia.

Although this is a conventional business card for an optician, color has been used to make a visual joke - the optician is based in Italy , and therefore, logically the eyes have been colored brown. But for the English practice the eyes on the card are colored blue!

Credits

▲ I would like to give special thanks to the following people for their patience, interest and support during the creating of these books: Sue "Scissors" Ilsley, Sue Brownlow, Deborah Richardson and Ian Wright.

DALE RUSSELL

The author and publishers have made every effort to identify the copyright owners of the pictures used in this book; they apologize for any omissions and would like to thank the following:

KEY: l=left, r=right; t=top; b=bottom; c=center

p13: The Bridgeman Art Library/Coll: Roudinesco, Paris Fabbri/©DACS 1989.

p14: (tc) Designed by Alan Fletcher, Pentagram; (tr) Masatoshi Toda/Graphic-sha Publishing Co., Ltd, Japan; (br) Designed by John McConnell, Pentagram.

p15: (1) Designed by Colin Forbes, Pentagram; The Face magazine, London; (tc) Designed by Mervyn Kurlansky, Pentagram; (cl) Designed by John McConnell, Pentagram; (cr) Alan Chan Design Co., Hong Kong; (r) Newell and Sorrell.

p16: (tl) Saatchi & Saatchi International; (bl) Designed by David Hillman, Pentagram; (r) Shin Matsunaga Design Inc. Tokyo.

p17: (tl) Lynx; (bl) Designed by Alan Fletcher, Pentagram; (tc) HDM Dechy, Brussels; (bc) Designed by David Hillman, Pentagram; (tr) The Small Back Room plc, Autran & Seita Ltd; (br) Bartle Bogle Hegarty Ltd., London.

p18: (tl) Gold Greenless Trott Advertising Limited; Art Directors Keith Courtney, Gordon Smith: Photographer Desmond Burdon; (bl) Jenner Keating Becker Reay; (tr) Newell and Sorrell; (br) Michael Peters & Partners Ltd.

p19: (tl) Michael Nash Associates; (tr) Newell and Sorrell; (bl) Swatch AG, Biel; (c) Minale Tattersfield and Partners International Design Group; (bc) Rowntree Mackintosh Confectionery Ltd.

p20: (t) Sunday Times Magazine; (br) Trickett & Webb Limited, London.

p21: (tl) Faber and Faber Limited; Pentagram Design Ltd; Cover by Huntley/Muir; (tc) Newell & Sorrell/Royal Mail Stamps; (tr) Alan Chan Design Co., Hong Kong; (cb) Neville Brody Graphic Design, London.

p38: (tl) Young & Rubicam Ltd: Art Director John Crittenden: Photographer Tim Brown; (bl) Illustration by Steve Russell; (r) Designed by Etsushi Kiyohara, Japan.

p39: (l) The Observer Newspaper, London; (tc) Designed by U.G. Sato, Japan; (tr) Designed by David Hillman, Pentagram; (b) TBWA Limited, London.

p52: (l) Illustration by Sally Kennington; Photographer Charles Settrington; (tr) Roberto Verinno, Barcelona: Photographer Paco Navarro; (br) Minale Tattersfield and Partners International Design Group.

p53: (l) Fitch RS plc; (tr) Saatchi & Saatchi Advertising; (br) Designed by John McConnell, Pentagram.

p66: (l) Emigre magazine, California; Cover Design by Rudy Vanderlans: Photography by Nigel Grierson; (tr) Quarto Publishing plc, London; (br) The Small Back Room PLC, London.

p67: (tl) The Small Back Room PLC, London; (tr) Illustration by Steve Russell; (br) Designed by Mervyn Kurlansky, Pentagram.

p84: (l) Quarto Publishing plc; (tr) Michael Mabry, Michael Mabry Design, Inc., San Francisco; (br) Newell and Sorrell/Royal Mail Stamps.

p85: (r) Neville Brody Graphic Design, London; (l) Giant Limited, London.

p94: (bl) Designed by Colin Forbes, Pentagram; (tl) Saatchi & Saatchi International; (tr) Saatchi & Saatchi Advertising; (br) Produced by Paul Barker & Associates Ltd: Art Director Tony Hardcastle: Photographer George Logan.

p95: (tl) Designed by Mervyn Kurlansky, Pentagram; (tr) Minale Tattersfield and Partners International Design Group; (bl) Designed by David Hillman, Pentagram; (br) I-D magazine, London.

p100: (l) "Coca-Cola" and "Coke" are registered trademarks which identify the same product of the Coca-Cola Company; (cr) Saatchi & Saatchi International; (tr) Designed by Spero Communication and Saatchi & Saatchi Advertising; (br) Saatchi & Saatchi International.

p101: (bl) Saatchi & Saatchi International; (tr) Saatchi & Saatchi Advertising; (br) Saatchi & Saatchi Advertising.

p114: (tl) Saatchi & Saatchi Advertising; (tr) Designed by Smith & Milton Ltd; (bl) Saatchi & Saatchi Advertising; (br) Saatchi & Saatchi Advertising.

p115: (tl) Neville Brody Graphic Design, London; (r) Grundy & Northedge, London; (bl) Minale Tattersfield and Partners International Design Group.

p128: (t) Saatchi & Saatchi International; Illustration by Peregrine Roskilly, Photographer Charlie Stebbings; (b) p129: (1) Illustrations by Kate Stephens; (r) Fitch RS plc.

p142: (tl) Giant Limited, London; (tr) Rhythm King Records, London; (b) Saatchi & Saatchi International.

p143: (tl) Minale Tattersfield and Partners International Design Group; (bl) The Small Back Room PLC; (r) Designed by David Hillman, Pentagram.

"I'd love it if it were pink, but red is vulgar."

Marie Laurencin quoted René Gimpel
Diary of an Art Dealer